TAXATION
WITH
REPRESENTATION

TAXATION
WITH
REPRESENTATION

ADVICE FROM A TAX RESOLUTION SPECIALIST

PATRICK LECLAIRE

Published by Advantage, Charleston, South Carolina.
Member of Advantage Media Group.

ADVANTAGE is a registered trademark, and the Advantage colophon is a trademark of Advantage Media Group, Inc.

Printed in the United States of America.

10 9 8 7 6 5 4 3 2 1

ISBN: 978-1-59932-848-5
LCCN: 2017942400

Cover design by Katie Biondo.
Layout design by Megan Elger.

This publication is designed to provide accurate and authoritative information in regard to the subject matter covered. It is sold with the understanding that the publisher is not engaged in rendering legal, accounting, or other professional services. If legal advice or other expert assistance is required, the services of a competent professional person should be sought.

Advantage Media Group is proud to be a part of the Tree Neutral® program. Tree Neutral offsets the number of trees consumed in the production and printing of this book by taking proactive steps such as planting trees in direct proportion to the number of trees used to print books. To learn more about Tree Neutral, please visit **www.treeneutral.com.**

Advantage Media Group is a publisher of business, self-improvement, and professional development books. We help entrepreneurs, business leaders, and professionals share their Stories, Passion, and Knowledge to help others Learn & Grow. Do you have a manuscript or book idea that you would like us to consider for publishing? Please visit advantagefamily.com or call **1.866.775.1696.**

To Vannie, the cornerstone of my life.

FOREWORD

When I first met Patrick LeClaire, what struck me most about him was his innate humanity and genuine caring, not only for his own family, but for other people and their welfare as well.

When I read *Taxation with Representation* (a title I love because it reminds us that every taxpayer has rights, regardless of what the IRS may be demanding), I was struck by his passion for citizens' rights. More importantly, I was struck by his extensive knowledge and experience in helping ordinary citizens resolve tax situations that have either been thrust upon them by their own unfortunate mistakes or, at times, by unforeseen circumstances.

Fortunately, I have never had a run-in with the IRS myself and have always considered myself fairly knowledgeable about how to stay out of tax trouble. But after reading this book, I realize how much I don't know about our ever-changing tax laws, red flags that could draw unwanted attention to myself and my business, and especially my rights as a taxpayer. I also didn't realize that there is such a thing as a certified tax resolution specialist who is authorized directly by the IRS to deal with IRS agents and represent taxpayers who have issues. I always thought that if I had a tax issue, my accountant would be able to handle it for me. I now realize that accountants often run into the same brick walls that we ordinary citizens do. What an eye-opener!

Being a current business owner myself, as well as a former Realtor® where I had to pay estimated taxes as an independent contractor, I now see how any taxpayer or business owner can get into trouble with the IRS unless they are aware of what to do, how to do it, and even when to do it.

Whether you believe you have a tax issue or not, do yourself (and your business, if you own one) a favor and read *Taxation with Representation*. If you are already in the throes of a tax issue requiring resolution, I urge you to give Patrick LeClaire a call. You could not find a more knowledgeable, experienced, and yet human and empathetic advocate to help you through the troubled waters of an IRS investigation.

Then do your friends and family members a favor (especially if they own a business or work as an independent contractor) and encourage them to read this book and incorporate its advice into their daily practices. I won't try to summarize all the great advice offered here, but I believe in my heart that if you follow Patrick LeClaire's advice, you will be able to avoid the heartache of having to go through anything like the troubles illustrated through his many stories of clients and colleagues who have had to deal with the IRS on complex tax issues. You may even be surprised to see yourself in a few of them.

Let's face it: We all need a lot of hard work and a bit of luck in order to thrive in business and in life. But when it comes to taxes and the IRS, you need more than hard work and luck—you need knowledge.

So, while I wish you much luck and success as you travel this road, I know that you will have a much easier journey if you arm yourself with the knowledge offered in this book and stay out of the sights of the IRS.

Here's to your (tax) health!

—Sandy Geroux, M.S.

ABOUT THE AUTHOR

Tax resolution expert Patrick LeClaire is the founder of New Life Tax Resolution. For over twenty years, he has been helping individuals with tax issues in Orlando, Florida, and surrounding communities. He founded his company to help people get their lives back in balance by solving tax problems personally, efficiently, and professionally.

Patrick holds a bachelor's degree in accounting from Orlando College and a bachelor's in human resources management from Spring Arbor University. He is an enrolled agent and a Certified Management Accountant (CMA). He is also a member of the Institute of Management Accountants Leadership Academy as well as the American Society of Tax Problem Solvers (ASTPS).

When Patrick is not leading his tax resolution firm, he is singing acoustic-based songs and playing his guitar with friends. He has been playing for over two decades. He's also a passionate traveler, taking an international trip every two to three years.

TABLE OF CONTENTS

FOREWORD vii

ABOUT THE AUTHOR xi

INTRODUCTION 1
Nobody Loves Taxes Except the Tax Guy

PART I: Getting Informed and Prepared

CHAPTER 1 9
You Can't Avoid Taxes,
but You Can Avoid Trouble

CHAPTER 2 27
Meet Your Business's Tax Department

CHAPTER 3 39
Consider the "Personal" in Income Tax

CHAPTER 4 47
What You Need to Know About the IRS

PART II: Responding to "Issues"

CHAPTER 5 63
Don't Fear the IRS—Make It Your Ally

CHAPTER 6 75
Planning a Strategy for
Dealing with the IRS

CHAPTER 7 89

Tax Resolutions—Better than
New Year's Resolutions

PART III: Getting Help

CHAPTER 8 99

When You Know You're Not Going
to Fix the Problem Yourself

CHAPTER 9 107

Trust Fund Penalties Require
Professional Help

CHAPTER 10 123

Being Treated Like a Criminal

CHAPTER 11 131

Taxation with Proper Representation

CONCLUSION 141

New Life Tax Resolution

GLOSSARY 143

Nobody Loves Taxes Except the Tax Guy

I spend a lot of time with people in trouble. My job involves representing taxpayers with tax problems in front of the Internal Revenue Service. If that sounds scary to you, you'll find this book helpful in allaying your fears. This is a book for people in business to learn systems, techniques, and approaches to avoid tax trouble or to control any damage that it's too late to prevent.

How I Became the Tax Guy

I grew up in a rural community where those of us who wanted to attend college and find work outside a farm or factory had to move to a bigger city. After my wife, Vannie, and I got married, we packed up and left for college, where I studied accounting. When I graduated and started to look for jobs, I realized that I didn't have a dad or an uncle or anyone else who was connected. My college was a good Christian school, but not in the top tier where graduates are recruited by businesses and accounting firms. My accounting professor suggested that small business could be my route to success, especially if I were willing to do the things that nobody else wants to do. What I soon realized was that most people I came in contact with didn't want to do taxes. They were afraid of taxes or thought taxes were too boring. Becoming the tax guy was not going to help them rise to CEO or even CFO. But for me, it led to a fulfilling career where I could really help people.

First, I needed some credentials beyond my bachelor's of science in accounting. Because I had a wife, an old car, a house payment, and about $40,000 in student loan debt, I couldn't afford to get my CPA or continue on to get a master's degree. So, I started working in small companies to get some experience. I worked with real estate and short-term rental companies but still wasn't making enough to get out of debt and pay for more education. That's when I found Adventist Care Centers, a faith-based, not-for-profit, long-term care organization in Orlando, Florida, that needed a tax guy. The organization provides administrative support and services to a multistate network of nursing and rehab facilities. Choosing to specialize in taxes had gotten me a job at a large, prestigious corporation, because I was taking the work that nobody else wanted to do.

After about twelve years, we got ourselves a CFO, Ron Wehtje, who was really something special and who encouraged my professional growth. I had job security and some good side tax work, but I still wanted more professional credentials. Ron came to me and offered the organization's help paying for continuing education. I said to him, "I could go for this certified public accounting designation, but I think there is a new emerging designation—certified management accountant—that's going to bring together accounting rules into a global framework." I said, "I think this is the way of the future," and he said, "You know, I think you've got something going on here, kid." He paid for a prep course, books, and exams, and lightened my workload a little bit, and I became a CMA.

After I graduated, I bombarded Ron with ideas on how we could improve the processes within the organization. I wanted to build out the accounting department and its tax section within Adventist Care Centers—and more.

Everyone Deserves a Tax Resolution Ally

Hooked on professional growth, I took a deep dive into taxes, including complex issues for the corporate office, Adventist Health Systems. Tax attorneys at the top corporate level encouraged me to take on more tax responsibilities, because they felt I knew my stuff. After passing three rigorous sets of tests to become a CMA, I went on to become an **enrolled agent.**

> *An enrolled agent is a person who has earned the privilege of representing taxpayers before the Internal Revenue Service by either passing a three-part comprehensive IRS test covering individual and business tax returns, or through experience as a former IRS employee. Enrolled agent status is the highest credential the IRS awards. Individuals who obtain this elite status must adhere to ethical standards and complete 72 hours of continuing education courses every three years. Enrolled agents, like attorneys and certified public accountants (CPAs), have unlimited practice rights. This means they are unrestricted as to which taxpayers they can represent,*

what types of tax matters they can handle, and which IRS offices they can represent clients before.[1]

I was licensed by the United States Treasury Department to represent taxpayers before the IRS for audits, collections, or any tax issue that a taxpayer, a corporation, a partnership, or any entity might appeal, all the way up to tax court. The appeals process is a logical and necessary part of a tax system that uses fear as a motivator for "voluntary" compliance. Sometimes that use of fear leads to IRS and Justice Department officials abusing their power over the taxpayers who are in trouble, poking at their pain points. Just as in any business, there are tax collectors whose competitive impulses overcome their sense of fairness.

I believe in fairness, even in business, where one can wrongfully take advantage when one has the upper hand. I don't believe in using an advantage of strength, power, or knowledge over people to extract something unfairly from them. I believe that people in my industry (tax resolution and tax preparation) must discourage this behavior. We should fight to make sure the nation's tax system provides not only fair resolution of problems but also good customer service and more information than the taxpayers even need. Openness, not fear, should be the starting point when somebody is trying to get out of trouble.

Based on those beliefs, I decided that I wanted to teach people, as a community service, how to handle their tax issues: Don't start from fear, but start from confidence that you're doing the right thing and avoiding any issues. Then, if you do get into a little bit of trouble, you can handle those issues. Only if you're in full-blown trouble and

---

1 "Enrolled Agent Information," Internal Revenue Service (April 19, 2017), https://www.irs.gov/tax-professionals/enrolled-agents/enrolled-agent-information.

are not doing anything about it would I need to step up and say, "You should be fearful." And that's where I think our industry has fallen short, too commonly using fear as a way to sell services.

This may sound strange, but over time I've come to love taxes and the tax system. Having an analytical mind and a desire to be altruistic and fair and to live by Christian principles, I see this book as my way of giving back to the community. People can benefit by learning to be strong in many ways. For people in business, learning how to operate properly within the tax system is a way to be strong.

What to Expect from This Book

Anyone who is just getting into business, planning a start-up, or running a small business—from the independent contractor up through a medium-sized business with about $10 million a year in revenue—will benefit from this book. Is your business growing and you're apprehensive about screwing it up? In *Taxation with Representation*, I simplify what can seem like an ultra-complex process. I'll explain tax resolution in depth—in more detail than any other book you can read, as it's an area that gets only passing mention or a single chapter in most business books.

Anyone from the independent contractor up through a medium-sized business with about $10 million a year in revenue will benefit from this book.

This book differs from other books on tax resolution in one final, key area: I personally don't believe in using fear as a motivator, because it destroys the spirit. I'll certainly explain what happens if something goes wrong, because we're human, and things are going to happen. But my explanation isn't to scare you; rather, it's to show you how we can handle these situations.

From my office in Celebration, Florida, I help people around the country resolve tax problems. I do this full time, unlike some tax preparers who take on tax resolution cases only when they have spare time in the off-season. I get referrals from bankruptcy attorneys and divorce lawyers, for example, as they often encounter people with tax troubles. Spoiler alert: If I stand shoulder to shoulder with you, battling the IRS for a year, it's going to get expensive. I'll provide plenty of advice in this book on how to prevent costly errors, but you'll also learn that tax resolution requires time-consuming documentation and negotiations followed by sustained efforts to stay in compliance.

Working with people in business, I have seen firsthand the legitimate reasons why you might fear getting tripped up by taxes. You want to focus your time and creativity on your service or product. You can't afford a full-time tax department, and even if you and your bookkeeper took business courses and read business books, taxes are brushed off as something you hire an accountant to handle. Your small business may be self-financed or started with borrowed money, leaving no money to hire a CPA. Until you can justify that expense, you may have to set up your own books and systems. Does any of that sound familiar? I am going to show you some simple, but not simplistic, ways to stay out of trouble.

In Part I of the book, I cover some business tax basics, including the ways in which different types of independent contractors, professionals, and small-business owners need to plan and budget for taxes. We'll discuss taking and documenting deductions as well as techniques for staying out of trouble. Some tax problems are common and happen with what readers may find surprising frequency. Other problems we'll discuss are personal, in that they result from the personalities, behavior, and relationships of individuals.

Part II of the book, starting with chapter 4, focuses on the tax system, including an explanation of the IRS collection process and your hard-won rights as a taxpayer. What readers may find surprising in this section is my advice: "Don't fear the IRS—make it your ally." With its very comprehensive website, the IRS offers substantial tools to help people understand their tax liabilities. Their publications, worksheets, and videos tell people what to do and what not to do. Keep in mind that this is free information coming from an organization whose purpose is to collect taxes. The IRS is not necessarily going to work in your corner to help you pay the least amount of taxes allowed by law.

Part III, starting with chapter 8, involves situations in which people really may need to fear the IRS because they are already in trouble and haven't acted to fix the problem. There is a storm approaching, and maybe they think they can get through with an umbrella. I want to motivate them to get some real shelter.

Setting up a business the right way to start with makes this all a lot easier, so that's where we'll begin in the first chapter. We're going to discuss business structure, record keeping, and budgeting for taxes—the things you should, as a business owner, get informed about and prepared for before any run-ins with the IRS.

PART I
Getting Informed and Prepared

CHAPTER 1

You Can't Avoid Taxes, but You Can Avoid Trouble

I meet most of my clients only after they get into tax trouble. If I could travel back in time with them, I believe I could show them the steps to take to stay on a safe path. Let me recount how such a conversation might go.

A freshly minted dentist approaches me about starting his new practice. He is a natural salesperson, personable and persuasive, but right out of college and in need of advice about how a start-up business handles taxes, which he admits is not his strong suit. He wants to focus on dentistry and building the size of his clientele without getting bogged down in what he perceives as nonproductive work.

As a tax resolution specialist and enrolled agent, I tell him he'll be able to avoid tax issues with the IRS if he keeps a few things in mind and implements a few measures.

He'll have to pay quarterly taxes that vary based upon his income—a moving target. He should take every tax deduction and credit his business is entitled to. With proper records and documentation, he will not have to fear an IRS audit. I tell him how to use a simple, easy-to-remember calculation to figure his withholding tax payments. Using free or inexpensive tools and spending only a couple hours a month, it should be a breeze to stay off the IRS's radar.

By the end of our conversation, he's empowered by knowing he can avoid any large tax issues. In fact, he may end up with a surplus at the end of the year.

The key is being consistent in record keeping as the company grows. He may add employees or other professionals to his practice, and that will add an additional layer of detail to his business operations. As the owner, he should never completely take his eye off the record keeping and tax payments, or a surprise could be in store; but there's no need for that to happen.

As a business owner, this is the tax conversation you need to have *before* you risk any tax trouble.

Many Companies Have Tax Issues

Today's headlines are peppered with stories of smart people and well-financed professionals having major tax problems with the IRS. You hear stories of celebrities or business owners being forced into bankruptcy that started with a tax issue and escalated into disaster.

The IRS says that in 2015, it audited almost 3 percent of the business 1040 returns that had income from $200,000 to $1 million, which amounted to 51,151 audits.[2] More than $6.2 billion in civil penalties were assessed for business and employment taxes in 2015, the most recent year for which numbers were available for this book.[3] The professional association I belong to, the ASTPS, estimates that more than three thousand licensed professionals are employed working on tax resolution.

Preventing tax problems begins with structuring a business in such a way that it's as simple to operate as possible. The easier the record keeping and filing requirements are kept, and the better cash flow is kept in balance with tax liability, the less likely the business is to get into trouble.

Whether starting off solo or with employees, a small-business owner must decide on a business structure, which will affect tax filing status. Many small businesses are Schedule C filers, some are S corps, and a few are straight C corps, but they all share the same basic filing requirements when it comes to quarterly filings and payroll tax deposits. Whether they are truck drivers, dentists, attorneys, or some other kind of independent contractor, the owners of these small companies must wear multiple hats. Everything that needs to be done to get a business operating and maintained properly will end up their responsibility sooner or later. Burnout is a real possibility, as these small-business owners often work seven days a week.

When the time finally comes that these owners can relax a little bit more, it's also when the mistakes happen. When the cash flow allows them to start turning responsibilities over to others, they may take their eyes off some of the less desirable jobs to focus on what they love to do—the reason they got into the business in the first place.

2   *Internal Revenue Service Data Book, 2015,* Internal Revenue Service (March 2016): 23, https://www.irs.gov/pub/irs-soi/15databk.pdf.

3   Ibid., 44.

How Does This Apply to You?

If you recognize yourself in the description above, remember, you are the one who must oversee everything to have it done your way. Others may take advantage, or worse, through illegal activities, they may put you in a very difficult and expensive situation with the IRS.

It's important to let the nature of your business determine what type of business entity you form. Many business start-ups choose an entity based on advice from friends or colleagues without adequately considering the tax consequences. Each entity has its advantages and disadvantages. To make the best choice, many factors must be considered and evaluated. The complexity of this decision is beyond the scope of this book, but excellent background information is available on the US Small Business Administration website (sba.gov).

Your business structure has tax implications not only on how you are taxed but also on record-keeping requirements. With complexity comes the risk of errors that can domino into tax disasters. Some business owners mistakenly think a corporate structure will protect them from penalties for not paying their **payroll taxes**. That liability is discussed later in this chapter and throughout the book, because it is the US government's main source of funding and is therefore a top law enforcement priority.

WHAT'S AHEAD IN THIS CHAPTER?

- Having a Plan in Place
- Budgeting for Taxes
- How to Set Aside and Pay Taxes
- Taking and Documenting Deductions
- Connecting Deductions to Business Needs

 ## Gary's Story

A small oversight in paperwork requirements can result in big tax headaches. One of my clients was an Indiana business owner I'll call "Gary." Gary had several locations in different counties, each a separate entity. Through the years, Gary maintained a good record of filing and paying both state and federal taxes. Economic changes in the state ultimately forced him to relocate to another part of the country. He filed all the required documents to officially close the businesses.

After a time, Gary started receiving letters from the Indiana Department of Revenue saying he owed taxes. The amounts due, as estimated by the state, were quite high, especially with added interest and penalties. Gary tried calling the state office, but that only resulted in frustration, because he was given false assurances that it was a clerical error and was being corrected. Instead, the account was turned over to a collection company that wanted him to pay $150,000 in payroll taxes for a company that was out of business and whose former address was a building that had been razed. Finally, the state offered a tax amnesty program that allowed me to get in contact with a person who could make the final decision to end the attack on my taxpayer.

NOT-SO-SMALL HEADACHES

The US government has a somewhat complicated and expansive way of determining what qualifies as a "small business." Depending on the industry, the size of the workforce, and the annual receipts, some companies with more than a thousand employees are officially considered small businesses.

Tax problems can snowball quickly for companies that are too small to have their own tax departments but big enough to have significant payrolls. One of my clients had sixteen different locations, each with its own payroll account, but all handled by the same back-office staff. An in-house accountant oversaw tax preparation, but an administrative assistant handled the filing and payments. It's not unusual for big companies to try to save money by having lower-paid assistants do such work, but sometimes everyone is responsible, which leads to no one being responsible until something goes wrong. What went wrong in my client's case was that an assistant was not informed that the filing date require-ments had changed, causing all the company's payroll taxes to be paid late. Penalties totaled over $12,000. I got that waived, but the lesson was the same as my advice for any small start-up entrepreneur: Oversee all delegated tax responsibilities.

Having a Plan in Place

Most independent contractors are susceptible to changes in business cycles and surprises in the marketplace that make their cash flow unpredictable. Realtors, for instance, can have several years of good sales commissions and then a bad year. A truck driver's income can shrink overnight if his or her mileage gets cut. A dentist may lose an insurance contract that accounts for a large portion of revenues.

Attorneys may develop a backlog of cases that haven't closed as quickly as expected. Failure to plan for these cash-flow shortages results in forced choices: Whom do you pay, and who must wait?

I have found this unpredictable cash flow to be the biggest cause of quality businesses getting into trouble with the IRS. The next biggest cause is the owners taking their eyes off the business—perhaps due to personal or family health issues—and blindly trusting someone to fill in during the hard times. In such a case, what you don't know can hurt you.

Sometimes I meet clients who purposely delay payroll tax payments for what they believe are good or reasonable causes, as in the story below. But as chapter 9 explains in more detail, the government accepts no excuses for such action.

 ## Ted's Story

A contractor I'll call "Ted" told me that he had taken energy and time putting together his construction crew, so he was reluctant to lay them off when he didn't have enough work for them. If a job came along, he didn't think he could get them back. They were talented employees, and Ted was sure his competitors would hire them.

Ted also had family members working for him, making layoffs even more difficult. How could he lay off his sister and her husband, who just had a baby and had another on the way? Feeling hopeful that the next big job was close at hand, Ted kept his employees on the payroll and delayed paying his quarterly estimated taxes and payroll taxes. He thought he could pay a penalty and interest but get back on track with the money he could make by having his crew intact.

Instead, the IRS took action that deprived Ted of access to business loans and imposed a multiyear payment plan. Ted had to lay off most of his crew and is working hard on smaller jobs to make the payments ahead of schedule, trying to restore his business to where it was before his error in judgment.

The ideal safeguard against failure to keep current on payroll taxes is to build an emergency fund into the business budget. Let's discuss budgeting for taxes and setting aside money in a separate account.

Budgeting for Taxes

Most of my small-business clients are on the cash basis of accounting and should be. Unless there is a good reason for it, accrual accounting should be left to the professional accountants and tax experts. It adds a level of complexity that only a bigger business would sufficiently benefit from, for longer-term planning such as sales forecasts, budgeting expenses based on revenues, and cash-flow budgeting. Taxes must be budgeted for by all businesses, however, because the government collects taxes based on the cash method.

The simplicity of budgeting on a cash basis is beneficial, but we need to add a few fail-safes. My experience, confirmed by other tax resolution specialists I have spoken with, is that simply hiring a good accountant and a superior tax expert is the best way to avoid costly mistakes. The problem I see among small-business owners is that they either don't have the cash flow to hire two more professionals, or they have too many priorities competing for their time and money. Often they can barely afford a day off or a vacation. For those of you in a similar situation, chapter 2 offers free information sources to help you keep up with changing tax laws to supplement the evergreen advice in this book.

Payroll taxes are the ones most likely to devastate your business and your personal life. Pay them without fail, and your life will have many more sunny days. Fail to pay them for almost any reason, and the storm will blow up at you faster than you could have anticipated. The government *allows* a business to withhold money from an employee's paycheck to cover payroll taxes. Doing so puts the employer in the position of tax collector and carries strict requirements to send that money to the government in a timely manner. If you're late, you will pay a penalty and interest. If you are *too* late, they will come for you.

Payroll taxes are composed of federal income tax withholding and the Federal Insurance Contributions Act (FICA); old-age, survivors, and disability insurance taxes, also known as Social Security taxes, and the hospital insurance tax, also known as Medicare taxes. These taxes are generally withheld by employers from employees' paychecks and are also paid by employers and contractors in their tax payments.

Many people don't realize that the government will credit the account of the employee for payroll taxes even if the employer fails to remit these funds. Legally, the money withheld from an employee paycheck for payroll taxes is an IRS *trust fund*, and no excuse is acceptable for the employer to hold on to it. The IRS doesn't care that the contractor has a daughter's tuition bill and wedding to pay for, as you'll see in the example of Larry's story to open chapter 4. The IRS has the right to **levy** trust fund recovery penalties equal to the full amount of the unpaid trust fund tax, plus interest, against anyone who willfully fails to turn over that money as required. Some employers have been surprised to discover they were personally liable for those penalties even though their business was incorporated. In legal lingo, the tax collector is "piercing the corporate veil" by conferring the liability onto the individuals responsible for the trust fund. There is no need for further discussion on this point. Just make sure you remit what you have withheld.

How to Set Aside and Pay Taxes

Entrepreneurs talk all the time about how they got into business to do what they love or because they had a wonderful new idea, only to discover that the complexities of regulation and taxes are robbing them of the energy, time, and money needed to succeed. Try to talk to them about setting aside the right amount of money for taxes and making a schedule for payments, and all they hear is, "Blah, blah, blah." Good thing I can translate into their language.

I'll try to make it simple. Do you know how maple syrup is made? Taps are placed in many sugar maple trees so that when the sap starts to rise at the end of winter, the liquid flows out of the tree to be collected. The liquid is placed in a slow cooker that evaporates the water in the sap. Only after hundreds of gallons of liquid sap are boiled down does it start to turn into a pure maple syrup. The tax code seems similarly voluminous until someone boils it down to the essence, and it is the final product that's important. Do it right, and you won't be left with a bitter taste!

Businesspeople today have cheap accounting software they can implement with little understanding of accounting, but they do need to educate themselves to have a basic understanding of how to identify and handle business expenses. Below, in no particular order, are some things that trip up business owners:

Eight Common Business Tax Errors

- Failing to keep clear records to separate business from personal travel expenses

- Not keeping receipts for purchases and expenses

- Paying personal expenses from a business account

- Failing to report revenue on the tax return for which 1099s were sent to the IRS

- Deducting charity donations without following rules for verification to substantiate legitimacy

- Misclassifying employees as independent contractors

- Missing quarterly deadlines for the employer's payroll tax payments

- Not responding to notices received from the IRS

The next step is to take a percentage of each check the employees receive and send it to the IRS. Employers must do this at least quarterly, but for most it should be done monthly. While paying taxes is never pleasant, at least with this method you are paying when you have money. If you wait the three months until the tax deposits are due, the money could have been spent on other important things like bills, leaving you to quickly come up with three months of taxes before the deadline.

MONTHLY INCOME		*Percentage of Income Spent: 56%*
Item	**Amount**	
Income 1	$105,000	
Income 2	$6,500	SUMMARY
Income 3	$2,500	Total Monthly Income: $114,750
Other	$750	Total Monthly Expenses: $64,470

MONTHLY EXPENSES

Item	Amount
Rent/Mortgage	$2,800
Electric	$1,800
Office Supplies	$450
Office Phone	$750
Insurance	$750
Truck Payment	$2,100
Auto Expenses	$120
Line of Credit	$4,750
Wages	$38,000
Employee Ben.	$9,500
Truck Insurance	$275
Travel	$2,900
Miscellaneous	$275

Net Income Before Income Tax: $50,280

Annualized Net Income x tax rate $17,095

$50,280 x 12 x (.34/12)

Based upon projected annual income of $603,360, $17,095 should be set aside for income tax

ILLUSTRATIVE CORPORATE TAX TABLES

Taxable income over	Not over	Tax rate
$0	$50,000	15%
$50,000	$75,000	25%
$75,000	$100,000	34%
$100,000	$335,000	39%
$335,000	$10,000,000	34% ←
$10,000,000	$15,000,000	35%
$15,000,000	$18,333,333	38%
$18,333,333	...	35%

Monthly payments are not only acceptable but are also a less painful way to pay your estimated taxes. An accountant can help you calculate the appropriate percentage of taxable income that should go into these payments. However, to get started, I suggest that you use at least 25 percent for federal tax. If you're subject to state income taxes, you might use 5 percent until you or your accountant can determine a more exact percentage. Monthly (as opposed to quarterly) payments of this amount will also insulate you from rapid changes in taxable income, even if your growth explodes at year-end.

ROUGH ESTIMATED TAX GUIDE FOR SMALL BUSINESSES:

- Calculate all your revenue from earned sources. Exclude money borrowed by the company for operations or growth of assets.
- Subtract any business expenses from that amount. The result is your estimated taxable income.
- Put 25 percent of the estimated taxable income aside for tax deposits.

To recap, you must pay 100 percent of employee payroll taxes and the employer share of FICA. The rough guide of 25 percent of taxable net income each month applies to your personal income taxes.

An important fail-safe that adds a level of professionalism to a business at little or no cost is to maintain a separate bank account containing the payroll tax money (which belongs to the IRS) and any other money due to tax entities. Because that money cannot be spent on any other part of the business, it should not be in the bank account used for operating expenses. When quarterly income taxes are calculated and payroll taxes are withheld, having two separate bank accounts is a simple but somewhat foolproof way to keep spendable cash away from non-spendable cash. In our minds, the balance in our company's checkbook is money available to spend, unless it is in a checking account used exclusively for taxes. When you write payroll checks, simply transfer tax money due to the IRS to your tax checking account. That account is also a good place to keep an emergency reserve.

Taking and Documenting Deductions

Congress empowers the IRS to allow certain deductions with a goal of stimulating business activities.

Some examples:

- Special deductions for certain industries to stimulate their growth.

- Deduction of the full price of qualifying equipment during the tax year it is purchased, rather than depreciating the cost.

- Credits for low-income people to purchase health insurance.

- Credits for spending to revitalize so-called *enterprise zones*, such as inner cities.

- Tax breaks for companies that operate and hire locally.

It is not wrong to take every deduction that you are entitled to by law. Some deductions are criticized as loopholes for special interests, but others are broad-based. During the Great Recession, first-time homebuyers got a nice tax break, and other tax breaks aimed to help Southern states hit by a hurricane recover from the disaster. I'm not sure what stops some people from taking those deductions. Is it the fear that the IRS will disallow them? Are they thinking it's better to be safe and conservative? Or are they just unaware of the deductions? The rich folks in this country know that a cornerstone of obtaining substantial wealth is finding and taking advantage of every deduction to decrease the amount of tax paid.

If you use your home for business, allowable business tax deductions for your designated home office space include depreciation, utilities, insurance premiums, mortgage interest, and necessary repairs. If you use your car for business, keep track of your business mileage and deduct car expenses. Deduct retirement contributions for yourself and any employees, as well as the employer-paid share of Social Security and other FICA matching. While on business, you can deduct the full cost of transportation, hotel accommodations, dry cleaning, car rental, and gratuities.

Certain tax deductions may trigger an audit. Deducting travel expenses, cell phone bills, and home offices sometimes gets small-business owners in trouble with the IRS. When you're writing off travel expenses, bring an envelope from your hotel, label it with a name and date, and keep all your receipts. Or, if you are inclined toward electronic documentation, take pictures of your receipts and save them in folders named for each trip. Keep an itemized report of your cell-phone bill, and if possible, keep track of all business and personal calls if you make both on the same line. To write off a home office, measure the exact space used for business; then, figure out what percentage of your overall home utility bills are used in that space. Try to keep a home computer for pleasure and a separate laptop for business.

If you have a guard dog to guard your business inventory, it may be deductible, but you have to establish that it is an ordinary and necessary expense. The definition of "ordinary and necessary" can evolve in different businesses. For example, historically in this country, medical first responders have not been armed, so the cost of providing them weapons would not be deductible as ordinary and necessary. But if an ambulance company decided its medical first responders needed to be armed, it could make a case that times have changed and its employees need to carry concealed weapons. Before taking that deduction, the company would want to have some documentation that armed responders can provide potentially life-saving aid more quickly and safely than unarmed responders. The point is that any type of business should be sure to keep any documents that would help win a discussion with the IRS on less-common deductions.

A sometimes-overlooked deductible expense is work done by the children of the business owner, especially those in college. Say a business owner paid his daughter to build and update his website. As long as children are paid a reasonable wage for the work performed, that payment is a business expense.

When revenue growth allows, try to get a midyear tax-planning session with someone who can help keep you on the right track. The cost of the session itself is deductible and is easily outweighed by the potential savings.

Money not paid in taxes is money that can be reinvested into company growth.

Take any fear you have about taking the deductions you are entitled to and replace it with an easy-to-maintain system of documentation. Have it reviewed periodically, especially if it grows to become more complex and automated. The benefits of automation will never replace your oversight as an owner and responsible person.

Connecting Deductions to Business Needs

Proper documentation and record keeping will go a long way in avoiding audits, which can be devastating to the momentum of a small business.

Consider, for example, a real estate agent who buys fifteen door locks during the year and retains the receipts. Simply making a note on each receipt saying what property each purchase was made for will provide better audit protection to show the IRS that none of the purchases were made for personal properties. The underlying principle is that expenditures are connected to a business need, and business expenses must be "ordinary and necessary" to be deductible. The taxpayer must be able to answer the "five Ws"—who, what, when, where, and why—for each business expense in case of audit to get a favorable ruling.

You may have heard it said that the IRS is more likely to audit and pursue small Schedule C filers than a corporate conglomerate. That's somewhat true, but not for the reasons you might guess. Yes, the big corporations have lawyers and tax experts who debate and argue tax law over lunch in state-of-the-art conference rooms. But the reason the IRS is more likely to go after a typical Schedule C filer is that many such filers just make it too easy. History shows that they are most likely not to document and record transactions properly. Let's face it: While IRS agents enjoy making an example out of celebrities, the bread and butter of their activity is those of us in small businesses.

So remember to document, record the five Ws, pay your payroll taxes, and use my simple-to-remember math calculation to pay quarterly income tax deposits. Don't ever take your eye completely off the person you hire to keep your business records, tax deposits, and filings, because the IRS has choreographed a tax investigation dance. It's a series of steps designed to find someone in your company and hold him or her responsible. Since you don't have layers of lawyers and tax experts, you will certainly be the focus of the IRS investigation, even if you say it wasn't your fault.

🏛

You've now read my most important advice for avoiding tax trouble, but the next chapter will show you additional simple (but crucial) steps to take to protect your business from common problems.

TAKE ACTION!

- ✅ What you don't know can still hurt you—so get informed and prepared.

- ✅ Taxes must be budgeted for by all businesses, so be mindful of cash flow—the government is on the cash method for collection of taxes.

- ✅ The government will credit the account of the employee for payroll taxes even if the employer fails to remit these funds. Legally, the money withheld from an employee paycheck for payroll taxes is an IRS *trust fund*, and no excuse is acceptable for the employer to hold on to it.

- ✅ Consider that monthly payments are a safer and ultimately less painful way to pay taxes.

- ✅ Document and apply the "five Ws" to your deductibles.

CHAPTER 2

Meet Your Business's Tax Department

Several years ago, a company I worked with automated its payroll system. This company had been relying on an interlocking set of spreadsheets that worked just fine but had one vulnerability: The designer of the old system, who was nearing retirement, was the only one who really understood it, and if there was a problem, nobody else could figure out exactly what had happened. The company bought a new system from a technology vendor and went through the tedious process of adapting the off-the-shelf software to its specific needs. The company had to make sure its automated payroll system conformed to the tax requirements of its home state of Kentucky, as well as every city and county where it operated or where its employees resided.

Once the new system was up and running, it took a lot of payroll workload off the staff. But after a few years went by, an alarming error came to light. An employee reported that his personal tax accountant had discovered the company was withholding the wrong amount for his city income tax. The city had sent out a rate change notice (by mail in midsummer), but the company's system had become so automated, nobody was paying proper attention, and this employer continued to withhold and transmit the wrong amount of tax to the city for two years.

This story had a strange and fortuitous twist. The city had actually cut its tax rate, which rarely happens. If the missed tax rate change had been an increase, the mistake would have been more than an embarrassment. The company would have been liable for back taxes, penalties, and interest, not to mention the loss of faith among employees affected by two years of tax underpayment.

Under the old system, the person who handled the mysterious spreadsheets was solely responsible for receiving and entering rate changes and for keeping records to justify those changes. Now, responsibilities were shared between the accounting department at this small company (an independent affiliate of a huge corporation) and computer network operators at a remote headquarters. If a rate change didn't make it into the computer system, it never happened— even though it was recorded in the accounting department. With no one person responsible, a mistake in the process left everybody scurrying to examine their e-mails to find out whose fault it was.

Any business that automates its financial processes can take a lesson from this story: Someone needs to keep an eye on all the mundane tasks a computer can perform so efficiently that they become easy to ignore. Software performs only as well as the person responsible for putting in the data, and that's where I see businesses get tripped up on their taxes.

WHAT'S AHEAD IN THIS CHAPTER?

- Your Business's "Tax Department"
- Always Be Learning
- Other Free Information and Help
- The Odds of Getting into Trouble
- How to Spot Bad Advice
- High-Pressure Sales Are a Red Flag

Your Business's "Tax Department"

Huge companies have a tax department overseen by a CFO. If you own a small business or are an independent contractor, look in the mirror to find your tax department. You're the tax department, and it's as much a part of your business as the products or the services you provide. You may assign some basic recording duties to an assistant or a bookkeeper, but just like with the company in Kentucky, someone has to keep an eye on that work. The cost in time and money of having an assistant and reviewing that work is small compared with doing it all yourself, hiring an accountant, or paying later to fix mistakes.

"Hire an accountant" is the safe and easy advice for the author of a business book to give. My advice is that even a sole proprietor or partner in a small business should think like a corporate CEO, taking a step back to watch over all the internal activities of the company while planning its growth and future. At regular intervals, the CEO evaluates the company's needs and resources and decides when it can add staff or handle additional professional service fees. Maybe a full-time accountant is out of reach, but it would be a reasonable cost to hire a qualified outside accountant or bookkeeping consultant to take a look at your record keeping and suggest ways to simplify the process. This provides an extra level of security and can be quite helpful if the accountant understands the needs of the businessperson. If the accountant is a good fit, you can gradually add more services.

Finding someone with the right personality, knowledge, background, and availability is the hard part. As in any profession, accountants have specializations, and they understand some areas, such as taxation, better than others. Not all are willing to do consulting or add services gradually. But even for a business owner who already has a happy relationship with a tax preparation accountant, a separate consultant can offer objective information on your business systems. "Objective" assumes that you have been careful to find somebody who's not pushing a product—a salesperson in disguise. Asking the people who do your taxes for objective analysis would be asking them to critique their own work. They might just recommend that you give them more responsibility and spend more money with them for better services. A second set of eyes is better to catch any structural problems in your business systems or to notice anything inappropriate.

When hiring someone to prepare your tax returns, make sure you know the preparer's level of skill. Automated tax software can spit out a good-looking tax return, but it requires someone knowledgeable to be as sure as possible that a return has been prepared properly. Don't hesitate to ask about credentials, experience, licensing, and how you will be charged, if a tax firm doesn't offer this information.

Always Be Learning

It's important in any business to keep up with what's new, better, and cheaper. This especially applies to your tax situation, where the more you know, the more likely you are to learn to use tax law to your favor. To avoid getting overwhelmed or bored, make a plan to regularly learn a little at a time.

The IRS has made public its Market Segment Specialization Program (MSSP), which provides Audit Technique Guides designed to make their examiners specialists in different industries. This is the IRS's way of saying that you have been warned as to what they will look for in screening returns. So take the time to search the Internet for IRS and MSSP, find your business segment's Audit Technique Guide, and become knowledgeable. Guides are available for professions such as attorneys and ministers, for industries such as construction or wine, and for cash-intensive businesses.

The Audit Technique Guides are not statements of law or policy but instead give you information about how to stay out of trouble and what might be defensible in an audit. Just keep in mind that everything on the very comprehensive IRS website is designed to help the tax collector. I attend conferences where I find myself staring in disbelief at speakers from the IRS as they advise and direct taxpayers and their representatives in the audience to take actions that I know would not be in my clients' best interest. The IRS reported in 2015 that its website had 140,000 pages, so it can be a bit overwhelming but is still a good starting point in your tax education.[4]

4   "Facts & Figures," Internal Revenue Service (July 6, 2016), https://www.irs.gov/uac/facts-figures.

Other Free Information and Help

Our tax dollars also pay for the Small Business Administration, which has a fantastic website at sba.gov, with a section called "Managing a Business" that covers filing and paying taxes. It's the perfect educational resource for a business owner with few dollars but time to spare. The Small Business Administration also supports the SCORE Association, a nonprofit organization with volunteer business counselors (mostly retired) who want to give something back to their community. It's a good place to find real businesspeople who have something in common with your business—certainly in the area of taxes, something every business has to deal with. I have found the SCORE Association volunteers to be very giving and full of great stories.

Your industry association can put you in touch with educational materials and even a mentor you can take out to dinner in exchange for some priceless advice about successes and failures in taking deductions specific to your business.

I love libraries, and they have been my source of tax guides and reference materials over the years when I couldn't or wouldn't pay the cost of a tax newsletter subscription or reference book. Now it is often possible to borrow materials from libraries electronically. Just be careful that you're looking at the latest resources and not outdated material.

Another warning is that general business books often gloss over the subject of taxes. They generally aim to cover everything a start-up or a small business might encounter, but when it comes to taxes, they brush off the subject with a recommendation to purchase software, get some training from an expert, or turn it over to a professional. Taxes are very dependent on individual facts and situations, so a business book—or class—will speak only generally to tax topics.

The Odds of Getting into Trouble

Even those of us working in the tax resolution business are not sure just how many Americans get into tax trouble. There's no precise number, because tax issues run the gamut from easily corrected, minor slip-ups to hardcore tax evasion, for which people end up in federal penitentiaries. A dispute with the IRS that exceeds $10,000 is the usual point at which it pays to hire a tax resolution professional, so our profession doesn't see most of the cases.

You could call any mix-up with the IRS, including an outdated mailing address, a tax issue. The IRS says voluntary compliance has remained static at about 84 percent, but the gap between what is owed and what is collected is over $400 billion. By law, the IRS has a National Taxpayer Advocate who makes an annual report to Congress about how, with more funding, the IRS could better help taxpayers avoid or resolve issues. The current advocate, Nina Olson, submitted testimony in support of her 2015 report that said her office was helping taxpayers resolve more than 200,000 cases a year.[5] Those are mostly just taxpayers who asked their representatives in Congress to help them with the IRS. She tallied all the post-filing notices and refund delays that generate taxpayer contacts with the IRS at over 9.2 million in 2015.[6] Each year, some of those millions of Americans end up behind on their taxes, adding to those who already were in trouble from previous years.

Michael Rozbruch, a Los Angeles-based author, trainer, and entrepreneur who helped pioneer the tax resolution business, wrote this in an online professional forum in December 2016:

---

5   Nina E. Olson, "The National Taxpayer Advocate's 2015 Annual Report to Congress" (April 15, 2016): 4, https://www.irs.gov/pub/tas/Nina_Olson_Testimony_2015_Annual_Report_to_Congress-4-15-2016.pdf.

6   Ibid., 9.

"There are currently over 13 million people, (and the number increases every year) from Maine to Hawaii who owe billions to the IRS. People with IRS problems come from all walks of life, from doctors to truck drivers. They live in big metropolitan and rural areas. Businesses that get into trouble with the IRS include retailers, restaurants, manufacturers, internet companies, service companies, distributors, and professional practices. The amount of tax liability owed may differ from taxpayer to taxpayer, but regardless of where they're located, the one thing they all have in common is they are all suffering from the immense pain being inflicted upon them by the IRS."

Thirteen million people represent about one in twenty US adults.

How to Spot Bad Advice

Spotting bad tax advice is a moving target, because as soon as one scam is uncovered, another one emerges. Here are some common things to looks for:

- An invitation to invest in a tax shelter that will keep you from ever having to pay taxes or that will get you money back from the government. The pitch often claims the tax shelter is available to only an elite few, or the time is short to take advantage of it. This type of scam has been around for a long time but continues to capture smart people who get blindsided by greed or because the referral comes from a friend.

- Tax protesters—a small number of extremists—push the tired argument that tax laws are illegal and that there are constitutional grounds to refuse to pay. While you should run as fast as you can from such people before they ask you for cigarette money or bail, don't confuse their nonsense with playing by the rules and taking every single deduction you legally can to lower your tax burden to as close to zero as possible.

- A tax resolution company that promises you a settlement with the IRS for pennies on the dollar. While it's possible to get such a settlement approved in hardship cases, about two-thirds are rejected, so be skeptical of anyone making a promise.

High-Pressure Sales Are a Red Flag

People with tax problems have often fallen victim to high-pressure sales techniques by predatory companies. The companies found them by advertising on TV and radio, or by obtaining lists of people with tax liens. The companies would demand a large retainer and set their clients up on a monthly payment plan, but in many cases they failed to deliver promised services or resolution. These companies took advantage of the fact that many people with tax problems have other instabilities in their lives, lack motivation, and fail to follow up, return phone calls, and meet deadlines. Rather than helping these unstable clients with hands-on interaction, the companies would blame the clients for abandoning the process and keep their money.

Authorities cracked down in recent years and shut down some of the biggest tax resolution businesses. For example, the California Attorney General's Office pursued years-long criminal and civil cases to shut down the law practice of Roni Deutch, who was known on late-night TV ads as the "Tax Lady." She settled the civil case and staged a comeback. Another California company driven out of business was Associated Tax Relief in Los Angeles. Class-action lawsuits and state attorney general fines pushed J.K. Harris & Associates in South Carolina into bankruptcy. Politics has played a role in the fortunes of such companies. When the IRS collects more aggressively, businesses like these thrive, but IRS budget cuts have led to less aggressive collections, decreasing pressure on people who might have hired a tax resolution professional.

I think anybody who is in tax trouble should be wary of companies with aggressive front-end sales, but I can't emphasize enough that those with a serious tax issue—an impending seizure of assets or criminal charges—can't afford *not* to get professional help. They should not delay meeting with a tax resolution specialist but should also be wary if they are only given access to a salesperson at a business that seems more interested in marketing services than helping people. The enrolled agent, CPA, or tax attorney licensed to handle the actual representation should be doing more than signing documents at the end of the process and should be closely engaged with the client from the beginning until the end.

Taxation is a specialized area in which small businesses should aim to get regular professional services, even if it's only for a couple of hours or a half a day per week, or they should at least get periodic professional advice to avoid trouble. But free resources are available for business owners to teach themselves the basics that apply to their industries. It's a continuing education process, because tax laws and circumstances change over time. If you keep up and pay proper attention to what assistants are doing with your tax records, you can blissfully ignore the bottom feeders of my industry, and you won't need to seek out a tax resolution professional like me. That's OK; there are plenty of people getting into tax trouble every year to keep me in business. You'll find out about some of them in the next chapter.

TAKE ACTION!

- ✓ Accounting software performs only as well as the person responsible for putting in the data, and that's where I see businesses get tripped up on their taxes.

- ✓ Hire a qualified outside accountant or bookkeeping consultant to take a look at your record keeping and suggest ways to simplify the process.

- ✓ The IRS has made public its MSSP, which provides Audit Technique Guides designed to make their examiners specialists in different industries. Take the time to get informed.

- ✓ Be on the lookout for tax scams, including companies with aggressive, high-pressure sales.

CHAPTER 3

Consider the "Personal" in Income Tax

A client I'll call "Joseph" was single for many years and led an interesting life, traveling the world. He was young, talented with computers, and supported himself while overseas doing web development remotely for customers back home. I don't think Joseph either realized or cared that, even though he was not in the United States, clients were reporting his contractor payments to the IRS, and he still owed taxes to the federal government and the state where he had started his freelance business. But when he met a woman overseas whom he wanted to marry and help immigrate to the United States, he came to understand that his tax situation would interfere with his plan to bring his fiancée into the country, buy a house in the Midwest, and set up a legitimate business.

Joseph contacted his state tax collector, the California Franchise Tax Board, as soon as he returned home, and he found that his problems were significant enough that he didn't want to have to deal with the IRS directly. So he hired me. We were able to reassemble records for the fifteen years he had failed to file income tax returns, discovering in the process that in some years, he didn't owe any taxes. We negotiated an installment agreement that was less cumbersome than he feared, and by the time we got him back into compliance, he had bought his home, started his business, and prepared for marriage. Surprisingly, the California tax board waived its claim for his income while he was out of the country. And the IRS, which had lost track of him for fifteen years, apparently looked favorably on his willingness to voluntarily submit his current address, six years of prior tax returns, and a proposed installment agreement.

Once he decided to return to the United States, it was wise of Joseph to resolve his tax situation, because IRS technology is constantly improving, making it more likely that he would have eventually been caught and faced criminal charges. The IRS has access to information from many sources, from databases to tip-offs from a disgruntled employee or upset ex-partner. As I began working with Joseph, we knew what the IRS knew about him, because taxpayers have the right to request their "transcript," which is the entire file of activity related to their Social Security number. As a tax professional, I can download the transcript into a program that decodes the raw data.

This was a case of someone motivated by love, not fear. In this particular case, Joseph was motivated enough to have already been setting money aside to pay the IRS. And it's a reminder that ignoring tax problems can have a significant impact on the course of your personal and family life.

WHAT'S AHEAD IN THIS CHAPTER?

- Tax Liability and Family Matters
- Innocent Spouse Relief
- Taxpayer Rights Are Fact-Based

Tax Liability and Family Matters

One not-so-unusual thing about Joseph's case is the marriage angle. Wedding plans often lead one partner to prompt the other to straighten up tax issues first. That makes sense, because families are often affected by tax problems. In chapter 4, I discuss the story of Larry, a real estate agent who had his assets seized by the IRS just when he needed the money for his daughter's wedding and final tuition payment. When IRS notices about failure to transmit payroll taxes started arriving at his business, he kept it to himself, assuming he would catch up before anything bad happened. His wife and daughter got a nasty surprise when his bank account was frozen and his credit dried up.

"Borrowing" money from employee payroll taxes is the best way to get the attention of the IRS, and family members can suffer even when business owners do it unknowingly. When their companies start to grow, they may choose to turn their payroll over to somebody else to handle. Even if it is another company that miscalculates or fails to file payroll taxes, the owner is still ultimately responsible, under most circumstances, for the payment of those taxes.

 **Brian's Story**

Not long ago, a client called me from a pay phone in Los Angeles with what turned out to be a really disturbing story. "Brian," as I'll call him, said that he had been a victim of identity theft. Although he gave me few details, I assured Brian I could help straighten out his resulting tax problems, though that is generally a drawn-out process.

As time went on, we dug into his case and discovered Brian had been raised by his uncle, whose son had a checkered life. This cousin took Brian's Social Security number and filed false tax returns to obtain refunds. The IRS was demanding repayment from Brian, threatening that he could be held criminally liable for falsifying his tax returns. I said to him, "Look, this is a tough situation, but in order for us to relieve you of the responsibility, unfortunately, we're going to have to start out by filing a police report." Due to the family connection, Brian didn't know if he could do that. We talked for a long time about what could happen, and Brian said he'd call me back. When he called back, Brian said he had talked to his uncle and his cousin. His uncle begged him not to file a police report, and his cousin promised to pay back the money when he got some. Brian asked me to try to fix his problem without his pressing charges. Not surprisingly, that long shot failed, because IRS regulations are pretty clear on requiring a police report to document an identity theft.

To make matters worse, the cousin concocted the refund scam using nonexistent children and the earned income tax credit, an abuse that is the focus of an IRS crackdown. To avoid a family confrontation over the possibility of sending his cousin to jail, Brian fell on his sword and settled the collection case by paying thousands of dollars that I doubt he'll get back from his cousin.

The IRS has been putting safeguards in place to keep people from claiming strangers' tax refunds. Brian's case was a little different, because a family member could easily impersonate him on a tax return and substitute his own bank account for the refund to be deposited.

Innocent Spouse Relief

The federal tax code allows married couples to file joint returns, in which both have liability for the tax and any interest or penalties that might arise, even if they later divorce. But what happens if one spouse earned all the income, filled out the return, and claimed improper deductions or credits or made other errors? It wouldn't seem fair to hold the other spouse fully responsible. That's the argument for a program called *innocent spouse relief*. It's not a get-out-of-jail-free card, but it's a way someone can try to make a fact-based case that she doesn't owe additional tax resulting from her lousy ex-husband's idiotic tax filing.

There was a tax case where a woman married a successful man and no longer worked. She cared for the children and took care of the houses and other assets. She had no reason to believe that anything was wrong. There was always money in the house account; she had access to it, but her husband funded it. When it was time to file taxes, she did sign a joint tax return but had limited understanding of how his business operations created wealth. He operated the business independently from his wife. At some point the IRS contacted the couple and presented them with a substantial tax bill full of penalties and interest. She discovered he was having another relationship, underreporting his income, and using the additional cash to pay for the affair. She divorced him, and the IRS still pursued her. Ultimately, the ex-wife was able to obtain tax relief because a court decided that she didn't benefit from the extra money that resulted from his not reporting income.

Taxpayer Rights Are Fact-Based

Another case that illustrates how tax law depends on the facts of the case involved "family" members in New Jersey. A mobster, just the kind of person the IRS is known to try to make an example of, prevailed in court by showing that the IRS had violated *his* rights. His tax attorney showed that the IRS used estimates and projections designed to produce the highest possible amount of tax, penalties, and interest. The attorney embarrassed the IRS with a defense built around the idea that unfair tax bills cannot be imposed on *any* taxpayer. It was a reminder that the IRS cannot do whatever it wants if people assert their rights, particularly the right to pay no more than the correct amount of tax.

A lot of people of varying character and circumstance have fought over many years to establish taxpayer rights in the United States. We've seen in this chapter how personal failures can affect family members and how the ability to overcome tax liabilities depends on the facts of individual cases. For those who get caught up in the collection process, it pays to understand how the IRS works and what rights taxpayers have—subjects covered in the next chapter.

TAKE ACTION!

- ✓ Be prepared for your income tax issues to get personal.

- ✓ "Borrowing" money from employee payroll taxes is the best way to get the attention of the IRS, and family members can suffer even when business owners do it unknowingly.

- ✓ *Innocent spouse relief* is the way someone can try to make a fact-based case that she doesn't owe additional tax resulting from her lousy ex-husband's idiotic tax filing.

- ✓ The IRS cannot do whatever it wants if people assert their rights, particularly the right to pay no more than the correct amount of tax.

CHAPTER 4

What You Need to Know About the IRS

One of the saddest cases I have worked on involved a real estate agent whose daughter announced her pending wedding shortly after graduating from college. That was good news, and "Larry," as I'll call my client, was so proud of his daughter that although he still had one final tuition payment due, he agreed to pay for a big wedding. Unfortunately, even for a good, experienced real estate agent like Larry, paydays are unpredictable. Larry's accounts receivable plummeted. To deal with his cash crunch, he delayed making his payroll tax deposits. He also ran up his credit cards to maintain his usual spending during the next twelve months. Meanwhile, notices from the IRS began arriving at his business.

Larry knew he was getting financially bruised but believed that once the wedding was over and business picked up, he would be back on track, and everyone would be satisfied. Just as the wedding day approached, the IRS froze his bank account. His cash and credit dried up at the worst time possible, leaving the devastated father of the bride crying, "Why now?"

Larry knew he had made a mistake but felt that because he previously had filed quarterly tax payments on time for many years, the IRS should have taken into consideration his business troubles and personal obligations. From the IRS's standpoint, it had performed properly, sending letters warning of the actions to follow if Larry did not pay the required amount. The IRS focused only on the fact that Larry was spending money on anything besides taxes, not caring that it was tuition or wedding expenses.

You'll see in the rest of this chapter that IRS collection powers, while formidable, are also limited and predictable in ways that are useful for taxpayers to understand.

WHAT'S AHEAD IN THIS CHAPTER?

- The IRS Collection Process
- Limits to IRS Collection Powers
- Taxpayer Bill of Rights
- The IRS Collection Challenge
- An Agency under Stress

The IRS Collection Process

The IRS has several forcible ways to collect delinquent taxes, but the process always starts with an **assessment**: a determination that the taxpayer owes a certain amount of money. The IRS then gives the taxpayer notice of that assessment, providing sixty days for payment. If the taxpayer doesn't pay or challenge the assessment within sixty days, a federal **lien** attaches to all property and property rights the taxpayer owns or acquires. The lien basically creates an encumbrance that stops the taxpayer from liquidating those assets without paying the IRS first.

People often confuse a lien with a levy, which is a way the IRS can actually seize property or money to collect what it is owed. A levy could be a seizure of bank deposits, or it could be attached to a taxpayer's future income. In the process of **wage garnishment**, the IRS uses a levy to require a taxpayer's employer to withhold a certain amount of money from paychecks and send it to the IRS to satisfy an assessment. Only when the IRS releases the taxpayer from the levy can the employer stop the garnishment. Wage garnishment is more common than most people realize and is an administrative burden on employers, who can be penalized by the IRS for any mistakes.

To avoid a levy, taxpayers who agree they owe money can make a payment plan to send a certain amount of money each month to fulfill the IRS assessment. But whether the taxpayer sends the money voluntarily or not, the IRS can collect interest and penalties in addition to the tax due. A payment plan may feel easier, but paying the assessment straightaway—by taking a loan from a relative, for example—can save substantial money in interest and penalties. If upper-level IRS managers approve, IRS agents can accept **offers in compromise**, which reduce the assessments for taxpayers who have shown they are destitute, for example, because of the burden of supporting a disabled relative or dealing with health crises in their families.

When a business has an unpaid tax liability, the IRS generally can collect by seizing property that is not necessary to operate the business. What often happens, though, is that the IRS takes an easier step and freezes the business's bank account, and when that action appears on a credit report, lines of credit dry up and the business has trouble getting any funding. A small business or an independent contractor can effectively be put out of business.

The IRS may turn a case over to its Criminal Investigation division if enough money is owed and/or if agents see what they call **badges of fraud**—behaviors that make the taxpayer look guilty. Taxpayers who take an unrealistically aggressive stance, refuse or fail to turn over documents, miss appointments, or get caught in lies are considered to have badges of fraud. Agents also find more subtle behaviors to be suspicious, such as the taxpayer asking if each question or each meeting will be the last one.

Compared to the total number of collection cases IRS agents handle, few get turned over for criminal prosecution. Though only a few thousand Americans a year face prosecution, it's a big deal, because the success rate of IRS prosecutions is incredibly high. Usually, when armed agents from the Criminal Investigation division come calling, they are looking for people they can make an example of. Based on news reports, you might think that Hollywood, rock, and rap stars are primary targets of tax evasion cases. In fact, the IRS will prosecute people from all walks of life in hopes newsreaders will see themselves in that predicament if they don't comply; a celebrity case just gets a lot more media attention. Putting a high-profile person in jail is an effective way to remind the rest of us to voluntarily comply with tax laws and to keep those playing fast and loose from feeling too comfortable.

It happens to them, too:

Timothy Geithner   Amount Owed: $34,000

Geithner failed to pay Social Security and Medicare taxes for many years while working for the International Monetary Fund.

Tom Daschle   Amount Owed: $140,000

He was a nominee to serve as Secretary of Health and Human Services, but he withdrew his nomination. Daschle failed to report payments to cover a luxury car and driver provided to him by a luxury investment firm. He claims he didn't think to report this on his taxes. He paid $140,000.

Thomas Hearns   Amount Owed: $448,000

Hearns's back taxes were from unpaid income taxes from 2006 and 2007.

DMX   Amount Owed: $1,500,000

DMX is an actor and rapper.

Abbott and Costello

Their career was already in decline when the IRS dealt the deathblow, with demands for back taxes bankrupting both men and causing them to split up in 1957.

Sammy Davis, Jr.

He owed nearly $7.5 million in back taxes at the time of his death. It took his estate seven years to work out a settlement.

Martin Scorsese   Amount Owed: $2,850,000

The IRS claimed that Scorsese owed $2.85 million in back taxes and related interest and penalties.

Minoru Yamasaki   Amount Owed: $537,000

One of the most prominent architects of the twentieth century, he was the designer of the World Trade Center Twin Towers.

Limits to IRS Collection Powers

Although the IRS has considerable means to collect delinquent taxes, its powers are far from unlimited. An easy-to-understand example involves home mortgages. Suppose someone owns a $1 million house, and the IRS places a lien on it to collect a $1 million tax assessment. The homeowner cannot sell the house without satisfying the lien. But if the house sells for $1 million, and it has an outstanding mortgage balance of $500,000, the lender is first in line to get paid. In that case, forcing a sale gets the IRS only half of what it wants, and just placing the lien may lower the home's value, because buyers and their lawyers and lenders are wary of properties with the encumbrance of a federal lien.

It's important for taxpayers who receive an assessment to respond within the sixty-day notice period they have before the IRS will automatically place a lien. The taxpayer has the right to challenge the assessment, make a payment, or show proof that the tax is unjust. Once the lien is in effect, the IRS has assessed penalties and interest, which will continue to grow over time if the case is left unresolved. The next step could be property seizure. But if the taxpayer contacts the IRS after the first letter and starts some back-and-forth about how much each side thinks is owed or can be paid and how quickly, negotiations have commenced. The IRS will put the collection on hold while digging into a taxpayer's finances. A revenue agent may determine that the taxpayer can start paying $300 a month. If that seems impossible to the taxpayer, it's possible to **appeal** up the chain of command to a generally more seasoned, more educated veteran of the IRS who has an interest in resolving these cases.

IRS managers are sometimes willing to be more flexible than the frontline agent, whose job is to collect money—period. Appeals within the IRS can go to an area manager, then a territory manager, and if necessary, all the way up to the IRS commissioner. Cases can be taken to tax court or the regular federal courts, all the way up to the US Supreme Court, to challenge something that might be fundamentally unconstitutional in the tax law. Big companies with deep pockets are most likely to take on such a challenge.

The IRS collection process is a choreographed dance, in that the steps are done in a certain predictable order set out by tax law. What's unpredictable is that human beings get involved in applying the law to individual cases. The agents have a manual to follow, but the agency will set priorities and go after some infractions more aggressively than others. Agents will stiffen up if they sense someone is wasting their time. And like any group of people, you're going to have the people who just want to treat everyone fairly as well as the people who like to see how far they can push and what they can get away with.

A former IRS criminal investigator I met told me that he and his colleagues were drilled regularly on how to question taxpayers, how to trip them up, how to get them to say what they don't want to say, and how to confuse them. "Some of these people I knew I could help, but my supervisors reminded me that was not my job. My job was to collect the tax. My job was to get that money," he said. He quit because he couldn't live with himself in that role. Some agents take advantage of a taxpayer's lack of knowledge or even a tax practitioner's lack of willingness to stand up for a client's rights.

TAXPAYER BILL OF RIGHTS

1. The Right to Be Informed

2. The Right to Quality Service

3. The Right to Pay No More than the Correct Amount of Tax

4. The Right to Challenge the IRS's Position and Be Heard

5. The Right to Appeal an IRS Decision in an Independent Forum

6. The Right to Finality

7. The Right to Privacy

8. The Right to Confidentiality

9. The Right to Retain Representation

10. The Right to a Fair and Just Tax System

Source: IRS Taxpayer Advocate Service.
For further explanation, see IRS Publication 1.

I insist that anyone who wants to be my client read the list of ten taxpayer rights. Often, people are skeptical that the rights are more than an IRS wall decoration, but Congress granted these rights with the force of law. The list is concise and easy to understand, but to see how it actually plays out, consider your right to know what the IRS knows about you. Suppose you get a notice about owing some tax money and you come to me for help. With your written permission, I request your transcript, a file that the IRS provides at no charge. The transcript will tell me everything that the IRS has assessed—tax, penalties, interest—and show any collection activity, possibly including actions that might be forthcoming in a month or forty-five days. Being warned that a letter, notice, or visit is coming is quite useful, because then we may have time to prevent or mitigate the intended action by the IRS, such as a seizure of property or assets.

Getting the transcript is a fundamental right and the cornerstone to starting any case on behalf of a taxpayer. But there's no law that says the IRS has to make the transcript easy to read. An enrolled agent like me has the access and specialized software to download and decode the transcript, which not even all tax preparers can do. Typically, someone who has failed to file tax returns is not a well-organized person and has a hard time getting information together. If that person tries to file a prior year's return with incomplete information and doesn't remember some income reported by an employer, the IRS calls this a badge of fraud. It's difficult to negotiate from that position. The unreported income will show up in the transcript, so that's where we start.

Sometimes the agent has files on his or her desk that don't show up on the transcript. You're entitled to that information too, but unless you get a cooperative agent, you may have to file a request under the federal **Freedom of Information Act** (FOIA). That little dance can be as simple as sending a letter, or it can get complicated. If the IRS is thinking about referring a case to Criminal Investigation, the agency manual says to have no further communication with the taxpayer or the taxpayer representative. The airwaves go dead, and you have to file a FOIA request to find out what's going on behind the scenes.

Generally, taxpayers have the right to contact the IRS and expect people at the agency to do their jobs. Anything less than quality service is unacceptable. Congress created a taxpayer advocate to stand up for taxpayers' rights. You can contact the advocate's office if you feel that you're being wronged.

Whether you are a pillar of the community or a mobster, you have the same right to pay no more than the correct amount of taxes and to challenge an IRS assessment. If an agent refuses to listen or makes every step difficult, that's a violation of the taxpayer's rights. Whether filing a complaint against an individual agent is worth the risk of making an enemy within the IRS is a concern, but tax representatives must stand up for their clients' rights.

The IRS Collection Challenge

The IRS was given a budget of almost $12.4 billion, including $4.9 billion for enforcement, in 2016. So how well does it do at processing about 200 million tax returns and collecting more than $3 trillion a year?

The IRS issues periodic reports with its best estimates of the "tax gap," which is the difference between taxes owed and taxes paid on time. The reports are not based on current data but provide the best available information on Americans' compliance with federal tax laws. A report published in 2016 covered tax years 2008–2010 and found no significant change in the compliance rate since the previous report was issued, for tax year 2006. Here are the key numbers:

- Average annual gross tax gap for 2008–2010: $458 billion

- Additional estimated revenue from enforcement activities and late payments: $52 billion

- Net tax gap for the 2008–2010 period: $406 billion

- Voluntary gross compliance rate: 81.7 percent

- Net compliance rate: 83.7 percent[7]

Year-to-year changes in the numbers are mostly a result of improvements in the estimation methods, the ups and downs of the economy, and the evolving mix of income sources, which have different compliance rates. Jobs in which taxes are withheld from paychecks and systematically reported to the IRS obviously are associated with higher levels of voluntary compliance. The IRS has to work harder to keep voluntary compliance high as more work gets outsourced in an economy with freelance "gigs" and increased globalization.

An Agency under Stress

The right to a fair and just tax system is important to individuals and businesses but also to the country as a whole. In 2013, IRS officials came under heavy criticism and even a criminal investigation when it became public that they were targeting political groups for extra scrutiny in granting tax-exempt status under the 501(c)(3) law, which pertains to certain nonprofit organizations. The scandal resulted in the IRS backing off generally from scrutinizing nonprofits' tax-exempt status, which opens the door to potential fraud. Weakening the IRS creates problems rather than increasing taxpayer rights.

---

7   "Federal Tax Compliance Research: Tax Gap Estimates for Tax Years 2008–2010," Internal Revenue Service, Publication 1415 (Rev. 5-2016), https://www.irs.gov/pub/irs-soi/p1415.pdf.

National Taxpayer Advocate Nina Olson, in her 2015 annual report[8] to Congress, addressed how the agency was coping with budget cuts by making cost-saving plans that "have serious ramifications for taxpayers and taxpayer rights. Most significantly, the IRS future state vision redefines tax administration into a class system, where only taxpayers who are the most noncompliant or who can 'pay to play' will receive concierge-level service or personal attention. The compliant or trying-to-comply taxpayers will be left either struggling for themselves or paying for assistance they formerly received for free from the IRS." Olson expressed concern that the IRS may be on the verge of dramatically scaling back telephone and face-to-face service that it has historically provided to help taxpayers comply with their tax obligations.

The IRS has been dealing with an aging workforce and personnel attrition, as an estimated four in ten frontline managers and six in ten executives became eligible for retirement in recent years. The agency has acknowledged that funding cuts, hiring freezes, and reduced staffing have resulted in fewer audits and less audit revenue. The IRS Oversight Board, an independent body that Congress created to provide long-term guidance to the IRS, explained in 2014 how budget cuts were affecting the IRS workforce: "New employees replace outgoing employees at a rate of one to five. This means a current IRS employee will see five coworkers leave, some of them the most experienced and well trained, before one new employee is eventually hired to cope with a growing workload. This puts enormous stress on new employees arriving at understaffed offices and those

---

8   The Taxpayer Advocate Service, an independent organization within the IRS, publishes its annual report to Congress online: taxpayeradvocate.irs.gov/ reports/2015-annual-report-to-congress.

who remain as they shoulder the burden of the work left behind until a new employee arrives to help."[9]

It's impossible for an agency in that situation to recruit top graduates. Those who are hired may find themselves reading scripts and making arbitrary decisions because of time pressures and the lack of mentorship by experienced colleagues to help them provide more nuanced and helpful service. The newcomers don't have the knowledge and authority to negotiate. Staff shortages lead to cases being dragged out for a year, or in extreme cases, two years. In-person meetings with IRS agents are on the wane, and reliance on new technology is increasing. The IRS has always gathered lots of data from many sources. A hundred years ago, staff went through newspapers to clip stories about newly rich people who might be living the high life and cheating on their taxes. Currently the IRS is expanding the use of data and analytics across the organization to find and understand patterns of noncompliance. That trend may help collections but not fairness. Taxpayer Advocate Olson testified to Congress, "I do not see any substitute for sufficient personnel if the IRS is to provide high-quality taxpayer service."

The IRS collection process runs on a strict clock. As soon as that first notice of assessment is sent, taxpayers begin losing rights if they don't respond within sixty days. But ultimately, the taxpayer is entitled to being treated fairly and a representative and an appeals process. Dealing with an agency under stress and possibly encountering inexperienced staff that can't provide clear answers, you have to know

9   https://www.treasury.gov/IRSOB/reports/Documents/IRSOB%20FY2015%20
    Budget%20Report-FINAL.pdf

your rights and have a strategy. The first step, which may surprise you, is making the IRS your ally, something I explain in the next chapter as we explore the circumstances, habits, and emotions that sometimes get in the way of successfully engaging with the IRS.

TAKE ACTION!

- ✔ Taxpayers who receive an assessment should respond within the sixty-day notice period they have before the IRS will automatically place a lien.

- ✔ The IRS has several forcible ways to collect delinquent taxes, but the process always starts with an assessment: a determination that the taxpayer owes a certain amount of money.

- ✔ The IRS can forcibly collect owed taxes from you through liens, levies, wage garnishment, payment plans, offers in compromise, and seizing property. Check out the Glossary for more on these methods.

- ✔ IRS criminal investigations look for badges of fraud and purposefully target high-profile cases to get publicity and make an example in the news.

- ✔ With your written permission, I request your transcript, a file that the IRS provides at no charge. The transcript will tell me everything that the IRS has assessed—tax, penalties, interest—and show any collection activity, possibly including actions that might be forthcoming in a month or forty-five days.

PART II

Responding to "Issues"

CHAPTER 5

Don't Fear the IRS—Make It Your Ally

Actress Melissa Gilbert is best known for portraying a sweetheart of a farm girl, Laura Ingalls, on *Little House on the Prairie*, a hit television drama that premiered in 1974. Ms. Gilbert hit the news in 2015 both for announcing her run for Congress in Michigan and for reportedly owing the IRS $360,000. The news reports said the IRS had placed a lien on her assets for back taxes she owed from 2011 to 2013. Ms. Gilbert reportedly said she ran into financial difficulties when acting opportunities dried up at the same time she was going through a divorce from actor Bruce Boxleitner. But because she had appeared on "Dancing with the Stars" during that time, she had plenty of taxable income.

When she remarried and relocated, moving from Los Angeles to the town I grew up in, she became the biggest celebrity ever to hit

4,000-person Howell, Michigan. So naturally, I was interested in her story. And you should be interested, too, because of the instructive manner in which she reached a resolution with the IRS regarding the large debt.

Ms. Gilbert apparently was unable to pay all the back taxes she owed at one time but was in a financial position to pay them in full over time, along with penalties and interest. In August 2015, her political campaign announced that Ms. Gilbert could negotiate a payment plan through which she will pay a total of $470,000 to the IRS by 2024 to erase her balance owed.

Ms. Gilbert, a former president of the Screen Actors Guild, remains interested in running for office. Her campaign said health concerns led her to drop her congressional campaign in May 2016, but of course the tax problem could not have helped. Her tax case typifies how even people who have substantial resources can get into a perfect storm of trouble with the IRS. Maybe she was dazed and confused by her divorce or couldn't anticipate where it would leave her financially in her life of uncertain Hollywood paychecks. But she seems to have discovered the best way to get on with her life, which I call "making the IRS your ally."

I admit the idea that you can make the IRS your ally is counter-intuitive, but hear me out.

Suppose you go to your mailbox on a beautiful spring morning, open it up, and find a letter from the IRS. Well, immediately, without even opening that letter, anxiety is flowing through your body, because the IRS never writes just to say hello and see how you are doing. You're going to assume something's wrong and probably be on the defensive. Once you bring yourself to open the letter, you may be intimidated by the fact that the half-page of information about your taxes is accompanied by five-and-a-half pages of dense documentation to cover every complication that ever occurred to anybody, anywhere.

An IRS letter is intimidating because, first of all, it's official and not phrased in a friendly, relaxing way. It's usually a demand letter. If it's not demanding money, it's demanding information, and people don't know what to do. They sit at the table, they look at that letter, and they contact a spouse, sibling, or Mom to ask, "What should I do?" Or worse, they're embarrassed because they did something wrong, and they don't tell anybody. Someone with no support system may take that letter and just stuff it in a drawer and not do anything, because with fear often comes procrastination. The delusion is that if you don't see it, it's not real.

WHAT'S AHEAD IN THIS CHAPTER?

- Fear and Delay
- Get Ahead of the Problem
- Get the Money from Somewhere
- Mistakes to Avoid
- How to Make the IRS Your Ally

Fear and Delay

Procrastination is the cornerstone of my business. Almost all of my prospects have delayed responding to tax problems, because they wouldn't be in trouble in the first place if they had been timely taxpayers. Some of the procrastination is fear-based, and some is from lack of understanding the consequences.

For example, some people file a tax return without making the necessary payment because they don't have the money at the time. They know they will eventually hear from the IRS and figure they will pay when that time comes, but then they are surprised by the amount of penalties and interest. Then the fear sets in and instead of calling the IRS, they do nothing, or they try to work around the IRS to solve the problem. They turn to the Internet for information or go to an accountant or anybody they know who might know what to do.

Unless they go to a tax resolution specialist, whomever they turn to might just deepen their fear. The person they contact says, "You're in trouble, man. You need to do something about this," but without any specific solutions, so procrastination's the easiest thing for them to do. They think, "You can't do something wrong if you don't do anything, right?"

Reluctance to give the IRS a timely response could stem from various causes. Some of it is based in overblown fear of the tax agency as a dangerous and prying Big Brother. Procrastinators may be afraid to admit they are guilty or, if they made an honest mistake, that they cannot pay. They may not understand they have certain rights, as you learned in the previous chapter. IRS agents are constrained by law. They're not going to take your home. They're not going to take food off your table. They're not going to make you skip medical care or deny your children medicine so that you can pay your taxes. They're not going to seize federal disability retirement benefits.

A tax representative who is knowledgeable about what to do and won't be intimidated by the IRS is the best hope for these procrastinators.

Get Ahead of the Problem

We've already discussed how some businesspeople, who should have at least a basic understanding of taxes, recklessly get behind on their payroll taxes when their cash flow dries up. They prioritize meeting short-term operating expenses, such as paying and retaining staff, instead of submitting required payroll taxes. Then the IRS notices, and company executives start hiring lawyers and pointing fingers.

And we have seen how people get into individual tax problems because of substance abuse, health issues, or disrupted personal lives such as a traumatic divorce or moving across the country. With the exception of active military on deployment overseas or documented disability, the IRS is not going to give a lot of leeway for excuses.

A company or a person can have years of pristine tax records and something can still go wrong. The company hires an embezzler, or the individual in charge of taxes gets preoccupied caring for a dying relative. And then one day a letter from the IRS arrives, and they're in deep trouble. That's why I am careful not to make judgments of the people who come to me for tax representation.

Instead, I help them understand the right ways and wrong ways to get ahead of the problem. For example, here are two wrong ways:

- "Pyramiding" of employment taxes is when a business withholds taxes from its employees but intentionally fails to remit them to the IRS. Businesses involved in pyramiding frequently file for bankruptcy to discharge the liabilities accrued and then start a new business under a different name and begin a new scheme.

- When a company that expects a tax seizure sells all its assets to another company for below market value and the people who got into the tax trouble open up a new company, the

IRS will examine the asset sale for signs that it was not a fair market transfer, without special consideration for price based on relationship or illegal intent. If it is not an "arms-length transaction," as a proper sale is called, the IRS will go after the assets aggressively.

When the IRS starts investigating either of these two types of fraudulent practice, typically someone involved will get counsel, try to cut a deal for self-protection, and give up the rest of the owners or responsible people in the company.

The right way to get ahead of a problem goes back to the simple transparency steps already covered in this book. Once a company begins trusting an employee or an outside contractor to handle its books and taxes, there should be oversight on those activities. Periodically, or whenever the owners sense something is wrong, an outside consultant should be brought in to go through the books and make sure that everything is being recorded properly. The outsider should review the tax returns and how taxes are calculated and paid. If the company is failing, sometimes it takes the clear head of an independent person—somebody who is just going to speak to the numbers—to persuade the owners to take the drastic actions needed to satisfy their tax obligations.

Small companies should do this kind of outside review even if they think they cannot afford it. It's a lot cheaper than hiring a tax resolution specialist like me after they get into trouble.

When a business accepts that it has a tax liability, we may reach out to the IRS and negotiate a payment agreement. But to have the IRS approve the agreement, the company has to also be completely compliant in all areas of taxes. All taxpayers making settlements with the IRS have to have filed all their prior returns, and they cannot fail to file and pay their taxes in the future. If a business is not going to have the money to cover both its tax obligations and ongoing operations, the owners have to take a long, hard look at whether they're a viable company or if they should shut down.

In other words, they now have to perform the same check-up they should have gotten from the independent oversight consultant *before* they got into trouble.

Get the Money from Somewhere

I worked with one company that fell behind on quarterly taxes and excise fees. Thankfully their payroll taxes were OK, so we had a little leeway to try to help them raise the money to pay the IRS. Since the company's credit scores were already ruined by the tax lien on its property, it had to turn to a lender specializing in high-risk business borrowers. The IRS had already refused to lift the lien temporarily to allow for a conventional loan, but the high-risk lender agreed to pay upfront the money that was owed to the IRS in return for complete access to the company's books and a portion of the gross revenues.

The interest rates were a bit steep but preferable to going out of business. The company satisfied the IRS, got its liens lifted, got its credit lines back, and was happy. I was happy because I negotiated it so that the loan proceeds covered my fee.

A delinquent taxpayer's best hope of getting money without paying exorbitant interest rates, I have found, is the old standby: family. I heard of a situation where a couple of brothers had a business in tax trouble, and when their father found out, he came in, read them the riot act, and then paid off the tax bill.

A person or a company can get a conventional loan to pay off a tax liability if the IRS lifts its lien. But first the IRS must receive a bond, which is basically an insurance policy that stays in effect until the liability is paid off and guarantees that the IRS gets paid off first from any credit line or mortgage that is opened when it lifts the lien.

Taxpayers in trouble who are hiring a professional representative should ask those interviewed whether they are willing to look for innovative payment solutions. Accountants and tax people by nature are very conservative about stepping out into uncharted territory, because they're afraid of getting sued, getting reprimanded, or losing their license. But part of the job of being a tax resolution specialist is to find the best way to protect the client. If I'm asking the client to pay me good money, I have to step as far out to that line as I can, even if I occasionally get pushed back.

Mistakes to Avoid

Since I mentioned helping a company negotiate a deal with a high-risk lender, I should make clear that I am not suggesting that similarly high-interest loans are a good option for individuals. Payday lenders are a swirl down the drain for most of the people desperate enough to turn to them and are a worse option than an installment payment plan with the IRS.

People who approach the IRS without qualified representation sometimes make a few common mistakes. I generally encourage prospects to initially talk to the IRS and see if they can solve their own tax issue before hiring me, but I also tell them it's important to understand and exercise their rights. They have to be prepared, because the IRS is prepared.

In many cases, people overexplain themselves, and the more they say to the IRS, the more likely they are to open up new avenues of investigation. What might have started as a simple fact-finding by the IRS over a small liability may open the door to an audit related to something the person brought up for no good reason while talking too much.

When a prospect becomes my client, I emphasize this to them: Do not talk to the IRS; do not write to the IRS; and if they knock on your door, simply give them my card, because I guarantee you that when you start talking, you're talking to people who know what they're going to say, they're going to listen to what you have to say, and it may not turn out well for you.

I avoid bringing clients into meetings with IRS agents, except in rare cases. Those cases involve people so unfortunate that the revenue agent has to see them and hear their story in person, because they can articulate their feelings in a way that makes it more human.

Three common mistakes already have been covered in this book, but to review:

- Avoid overexplaining

- Being overtly hostile to an IRS agent, not keeping appointments, and refusing to provide documents only invites suspicion (One taxpayer even threatened to blow up the agency's building)

- Trying to hide behind a corporate veil doesn't work when the IRS has authority to hold a company's responsible parties liable

Seven True but Stupid Taxpayer Excuses

Below are excerpts from some of the many incredible things Americans have written or said, sometimes even in court, to excuse their nonpayment of taxes.

- I suffer from Late Filing Syndrome.

- I'm not liable to pay taxes because I'm an alien (from outer space).

- I'm sure I paid. You must have lost it.

- I refuse to file as it violates my Fifth Amendment rights.

- I was diagnosed as having a tax phobia.

- I shouldn't have to pay the assessment because I never filed the tax return.

- I have voluntarily opted out of the federal tax system.

How to Make the IRS Your Ally

I have emphasized that when you approach the IRS to resolve a tax problem, you must be prepared and know your rights. And guess where you can go to learn what you need to know? The IRS website.

Keeping in mind that every product of the IRS is designed to collect taxes, the website is still a great starting point for understanding tax law. More importantly, it tells you your rights and how different processes will unfold. If you're planning to ask the IRS for a certain resolution, the website will tell you what to expect, including the likelihood of it being a viable option.

As soon as a company encounters a potential problem, a well-prepared call to the IRS can provide a sense of how the IRS will react. It can be hard to get through during the tax-filing season, but if you do, the IRS has basic administrative staff members who can direct you to information that will help answer some of your questions if they cannot answer them directly. IRS publications, available online, are a good starting point but cannot be cited like a law to support a taxpayer's case.

People are surprised they can actually have a conversation with someone at the IRS. Most of the agents who answer the initial phone calls are bureaucrats who happened to get a job there, with a decent paycheck and reasonable benefits. They're not bad people. They're trying to take care of their families, just like the rest of us. They know their job is to collect taxes, but they can be reasonable and, at times, helpful. If the conversation gets uncomfortable, however, you can just end it.

We've covered how fear of the IRS leads to procrastination and more trouble and expense than you'll encounter if you stay on top of your tax obligations and make the IRS your ally. You have seen that tax professionals can help keep you out of trouble or provide innovative ways to get the money or time you need to pay off a tax liability if you fall into bad habits or unfortunate circumstances. The next chapter explains, step-by-step, how tax resolution works.

TAKE ACTION!

- ✓ Make the IRS your ally!
- ✓ Procrastination is the cornerstone of my business, so if you'd like to avoid tax trouble, take action immediately.
- ✓ When dealing with the IRS, don't overexplain, be overtly hostile, or hide behind a "corporate veil."
- ✓ When the IRS starts investigating either of these two types of fraudulent practice, typically someone involved will get counsel, try to cut a deal for self-protection, and give up the rest of the owners or responsible people in the company. The right way

to get ahead of a problem goes back to the simple transparency steps already covered in this book.

✔ Part of the job of being a tax resolution specialist is to find the best way to protect the client.

CHAPTER 6

Planning a Strategy for Dealing with the IRS

To help you understand how I deal with the IRS, I am going to use an actual call I got and project how it might play out. I'll call the client "Jeff" and fictionalize the details to protect his privacy and show you some of the more predictable steps that occur in arguing a tax case. My process starts with getting to know the prospective clients and then finding out what the IRS knows about them.

Like many people who need tax resolution assistance, Jeff has a hard-luck story. He tells me that he is living on disability payments and can't make ends meet because he has a tax lien on his bank account. He'll soon be homeless if the IRS levies his income, which he calls disability payments but which might not officially qualify as such. My gut instinct is that Jeff is a sympathetic figure the IRS is not going to toss out on the street. He became disabled while working as a military contractor in a combat zone overseas. He was serving his country in Afghanistan, where one can easily imagine it was hard to keep his eyes on his tax returns. The IRS has policies to protect active-duty service members in similar situations, but the rules don't cover contractors.

To represent Jeff's interests, I start by getting his power of attorney and obtaining his IRS transcripts, a download of coded information showing what the IRS knows about Jeff, his income, and his tax payment history. Often, the written record differs from a client's memory. In Jeff's case, I believe he is confused about differences between his state and federal tax liabilities. His memory and record keeping still suffer from the haze of war.

Once I have examined the transcripts, I contact the IRS and get them to agree to a stay on the lien, which means Jeff can still access his checking account while we work out a strategy. His disability and service to his country help support our case that he should be allowed to recreate lost records using alternative methods for the years in which the IRS says he failed to file. We then complete his tax returns and hope they don't show him owing much money.

If the amount owed is more than he can afford, I will urge Jeff to borrow the money from relatives or friends. As a last resort, we will propose a payment plan to the IRS, but I will warn Jeff that paying over time racks up costly interest and penalties.

Jeff's case may sound unusually sympathetic, but keep in mind that civilians who voluntarily go to war zones are often well-paid and work for companies that are experienced at handling the details during military deployments. In some sense, Jeff is shielded only by broader protections, put into law by Congress, that keep a leash on the IRS. Lawmakers have not wanted IRS agents to become so aggressive that they take basic living necessities away from people.

WHAT'S AHEAD IN THIS CHAPTER?

- Retaining Good Representation—the Enrolled Agent
- Hurry Up and Wait—Settling and Appeal
- Everyone's Entitled to Representation
- Tax Resolution Takes Time and Money
- Misconceptions about Bankruptcy
- Hard-earned Taxpayer Rights

Retaining Good Representation— the Enrolled Agent

Once the IRS takes the initiative to collect money, you are on the defensive. It's up to you to shift the momentum through the quality of your response. Retaining a representative who is technically capable, is willing to fight for you, and has a good reputation with the agents can help. As a tax resolution representative, my approach is to try to convince the agents that you and I are going to meet our obligations, be friendly, forthcoming, and honest, and keep within the timeline. I will be persistent in fairness to both sides of the dispute. When the IRS is not getting its money, it wants to at least see progress toward getting the money.

You can represent yourself, but because of my license as an enrolled agent, the IRS has to give me priority access. Agents have to talk to me; they can't lie to me or mislead me. I can get transcripts quickly, decode them, understand them, and determine if we need to file papers to get additional case files. Simply knowing when and how to request a delay in collections can buy time to gather facts and documentation to strengthen our negotiations. Trying to figure this out for yourself as you go along can be overwhelming.

WHO CAN BE A REPRESENTATIVE?

As explained in the Introduction, an enrolled agent is a person who has earned the privilege of representing taxpayers before the Internal Revenue Service either by passing a three-part, comprehensive IRS test covering individual and business tax returns, or through experience as a former IRS employee. Enrolled agents, like attorneys and CPAs, are unrestricted as to which taxpayers they can represent, what types of tax matters they can handle, and which IRS offices they can represent clients before.

Enrolled agents, attorneys, and CPAs also can earn designation as a tax resolution specialist after testing by the ASTPS. I am both an enrolled agent and a tax resolution specialist.

Trying to show the IRS that we're doing everything in as timely a way as possible but also giving you time you may need to gather resources is like walking a tightrope. Maybe you want the time to save up money for a payment, but if the IRS concludes we are just dragging out the case, we could both find ourselves in trouble. The IRS could fine me for delaying a case, and my client could lose any goodwill built up over the prior months by being friendly and forthcoming. With my experience on that tightrope, I maintain the proper balance and pace.

Hurry Up and Wait—Settling and Appeal

While the IRS is strict about imposing deadlines on taxpayers, once we submit a case—even a proposed settlement that was negotiated with an IRS agent—it may sit for six months. The time involved depends on the level at which it must be handled. If you receive a computer-generated letter from the collection service and just want to pay what is owed, you can call or go online and have the case closed quickly. The IRS has call centers across the country handing off to each other as the day progresses across the time zones. The staff can answer general questions and set up basic payment agreements.

Agents are generally assigned to cases that involve businesses as well as those involving individuals with a large liability. Once you have established phone contact with the agent, e-mail and faxes are often used for the follow-up. When a case goes into appeals, different agents, who are independent of collections, get involved. In a complex case, I may develop a phone relationship over time with an experienced agent overseeing the appeal.

Suppose the case of Jeff, the military contractor, had gotten complicated. Since he filed no tax return in 2010, the IRS created one for him, called a **substitute for return** (SFR) based upon estimates plus interest and penalties. As is typical for an SFR, it was substantially higher than the late return I filed for him. Jeff told me he earned all his money through a company he set up as a subcontractor, but he apparently was also paid directly by a corporation whose payment record did not show up in our original investigation. Now the IRS was accusing us of falsifying our return. In the meantime, Jeff received a new diagnosis that traumatic brain injury was involved in the condition that sent him home from Afghanistan.

At this point, I would be keeping the agent overseeing the case (or its appeal) updated on developments. The IRS could take Jeff's medical condition into account as a reason to waive penalties, or it could investigate him further. If he posts pictures of himself on Facebook skydiving and drinking beer with the guys down at the country club, his disability hardship story is going to be hard to sell. The IRS cannot consider a lifestyle in general but can look for specific badges of fraud in making a negative ruling. The depth of investigation usually depends on the extent of the liability, but nothing prevents an agent from making a quick Internet search before sitting down with a taxpayer. I do the same as a precaution to avoid unpleasant surprises.

Everyone's Entitled to Representation

Because of my belief in the taxpayer's right to representation, my goal is to try to represent everyone who comes through the door. Those of us in tax resolution can represent known criminals in a case where their rights have been violated. But I won't represent somebody who wants help doing something illegal, and that includes tax protesters who want to make the frivolous case that all taxation is unconstitutional. I could find myself sanctioned or fined for wasting the IRS's time.

It's important for a tax representative to watch for warning signs that a case might lead to a criminal investigation. If I miss the signs, it's possible I could be forced to testify against my own client. But I have developed methods to see when a case is headed that way. I can then refer the client to a lawyer I work with to invoke the confidentiality of attorney-client privilege.

I will support our clients' legitimate positions before the IRS to the fullest extent of the tax code. I will defend them within allowed legal limits. So I will challenge IRS agents. I will go to appeals. I will go to tax court if my client has a legitimate position. You can read my company mission statement, which goes into more detail about how I operate.

OUR MISSION STATEMENT

New Life Tax Resolution exists for the purpose of representing clients before the IRS in all appropriate tax matters.

We will support our clients' legitimate positions before the IRS to the fullest extent of the tax code. We will defend them within the allowed legal limits provided to us at New Life Tax Resolution.

We will operate with Integrity, Honesty, and Vigor in all dealings with our clients and the IRS. We will treat everyone in a respectful and caring manner.

We will seek to present our clients in the best possible manner before the IRS. We will strive to reach a successful conclusion while operating within the framework of behavior established by the governing entities.

We believe the client is our partner and will act along with us in a manner that will support a satisfactory resolution based on facts and situation.

Our fees will reflect the professional level of excellence that we strive to maintain.

We will constantly update our skills in order to represent our clients effectively throughout the various stages of the resolution process.

We will communicate with our clients in an ongoing, timely manner regarding the progress of their case before the IRS.

We will strive to be good stewards of the community and will participate in and encourage the betterment of the lives of our country, neighbors, and friends.

Tax Resolution Takes Time and Money

All prospective clients sign an engagement letter to hire me first for investigation and analysis of their case. After we find out about their situation and what the IRS knows, we determine the strategy that's most likely to be successful. If the client agrees, we then sign a second engagement letter that says we are going to pursue the agreed-upon kind of resolution. For example, we might file back-tax returns or replace tax returns filed for the client by the IRS. The case might also involve identity theft or an innocent spouse defense, or we might make an **offer in compromise**, as explained in the next section of this chapter.

The cost of these services obviously varies based on the complexity of the case, and it can be substantial. There's a lot of hand-holding in this business, because many clients who have tax problems have other issues in their lives. They tend to be procrastinators (discussed further in chapters 5 and 8), and I need to keep them on track, not only for the full resolution process but also for the years that follow. When I meet with them to give them the good news that their case is finally settled, I have to say, "Look, if you sign these papers with the IRS, this is what you'll have to pay. It's a good agreement, but if you fail to keep in compliance for the next five years, you could be at risk of having the whole contract negated, and collections will become aggressive all over again."

At that point, I have come up with what I consider a reasonable insurance policy. For a small annual amount, I will pull a client's transcripts twice a year. I will look for anything that shows that my clients are failing to meet the agreement. I'll contact them to remind them that they're dangerously close to the edge and that, if necessary, we may have to work together again. If they fail to maintain their contract, and we catch it early, we can sometimes get a little bit of understanding from the IRS where they'll reinstate it. We can continue toward the five-year deadline.

I've heard others in my industry say that the noncompliance rate—the people who fall out of their agreements—runs as high as 50 percent, making for a good pool of repeat clients. The rationale is that people are responsible for their own lives. But I think that's a fundamentally wrong way of thinking. If you know ahead of time that people are at high risk of failure, it's unfair to wait for them to fail so you can collect another fee from them. It's ultimately up to the clients whether to accept or refuse the settlement and the "insurance policy."

I can rarely afford to take on pro bono cases, and too often, prospective clients decide to handle their own cases because they say they can't afford to pay for representation. I give them a checklist, refer them to my blog posts, and urge them to contact the IRS. Failing to reply to an IRS assessment is the worst thing they can do, especially if they have a potentially solid case to make. It takes a certain personality type, but if they just ask the IRS for a reduction, they might get a yes at the times you would least expect.

Misconceptions about Bankruptcy

Some business owners with tax problems mistakenly decide that bankruptcy is their best way to get a fresh start. To evaluate whether that makes sense, they should ask themselves these questions:

- Will bankruptcy have a negative effect on your business?

- Is the bankruptcy filing primarily due to an outstanding and large tax bill?

- Are all the taxes you owe dischargeable in bankruptcy?

- What amount would be acceptable to the IRS in an offer in compromise?

Business owners should avoid a bankruptcy filing if their reputation is built on trust and financial skills. Who wants a financial advisor or money manager who can't manage his own money? An offer in compromise would settle tax debt for less than the full amount owed and immediately have a positive effect on credit scores, leaving no record of a court case. The IRS decides who is qualified to make an offer in compromise and investigates the taxpayer's income, expenses, and assets to determine whether the taxpayer legitimately cannot pay the full tax liability.

If clients want to take the bankruptcy route, I refer them to a bankruptcy attorney but work with them to determine which taxes are dischargeable in bankruptcy. For example, the payroll trust fund taxes (which employers are required to withhold from employee paychecks) and sales taxes paid by customers are still owed to the government even after a bankruptcy. Because many taxes are not dischargeable, someone considering a bankruptcy filing must evaluate whether there are enough additional debts besides the taxes due to the IRS to make the undesirable process of bankruptcy worthwhile. The IRS will hold off on collections during bankruptcy, but once the process is completed, the IRS will present its bill. The IRS will go after the assets wherever they wind up. If the business has been sold, the IRS will look at whether it was a legitimate sale for a fair price to ensure that the owner was not using a fraudulent sale to hide assets.

The alternative to bankruptcy is to consider an offer in compromise to resolve the case with the IRS. But let's say we made a reasonable offer, and after six months of us doing everything the IRS asked, it was refused. Even at that point, where I realize they're not going to accept any kind of modified offer in compromise from us, we have options besides bankruptcy. If we believe the taxpayer legitimately cannot pay the full tax liability or has been assessed unfairly, we can appeal the case within the IRS or take the case to tax court. Occasionally, someone will hire attorneys to take a case to federal district court.

An appeal might prevail for several reasons. The revenue agent who originally considered the case might simply have taken a dislike to my client. Maybe my client or I offended or challenged him or her in some way. That slight should not carry over in the appeal, because there's a rule forbidding communications about the case between the frontline and appeals agents. Our frontline nemesis can't say, "This guy's a jerk. I wouldn't give him anything."

Beyond that, the appeals agents are more educated and experienced. They've got a case to settle. They understand what the agency's management is looking for. If we have a fact-based story to tell along with the supporting documents, we'll have a much better chance of success in appeals.

If you take your case to tax court, the judge's first step generally is to send it back to the appeals agent and say, "Hey, guys, why don't you see if you can work this out?" Having the tax court urging the IRS to find a resolution can work in your favor as long as you have a legitimate position and a representative who is reasonable, articulate, and determined.

Hard-Earned Taxpayer Rights

When we take a case to appeals, we are benefiting from a long history of many people courageously standing up for their fundamental rights to be treated fairly. Some people needlessly worry that they'll look guilty if they press too hard for their rights. In fact, Congress granted the Taxpayer Bill of Rights purposely to keep the IRS from becoming arbitrary, authoritarian, or omnipotent. If anything, the taxpayer's rights are underutilized.

If I find myself dealing with a revenue agent who has wandered into foul territory, I won't hesitate to say, "Look, my taxpayer has the right to quality service, and this is specifically what you have done that's interfering with our rights." My objection might not be taken seriously by a frontline agent, but it will be understood at higher levels of management. For example, if we find that our agent colored our case by improperly briefing the appeals people, that's a clear breach of the taxpayer's right to confidentiality.

An enrolled agent once recounted to me how he handled an audit in which he was told he could not represent his client despite having a valid power of attorney. He stopped the meeting and went up through several layers of IRS management, eventually getting a letter from a supervisor stating that it was a misunderstanding and there would be no further collection activity.

Our strategy for dealing with the IRS boils down to presenting the client in the most positive light and finding the proper negotiating partner within the agency to make a reasonable compromise. The next chapter goes into detail about how to get reliable help with tax resolution.

TAKE ACTION!

- ✓ You can represent yourself, but because of my license as an enrolled agent, the IRS has to give me priority access. Agents have to talk to me; they can't lie to me or mislead me. I can get transcripts quickly, decode them, understand them, and determine if we need to file papers to get additional case files.

- ✓ Those of us in tax resolution can represent known criminals in a case where their rights have been violated. But I won't represent somebody who wants help doing something illegal, and that includes tax protesters who want to make the frivolous case that all taxation is unconstitutional.

- ✓ Many taxes are not dischargeable; evaluate whether there are enough additional debts besides the taxes due to the IRS to make bankruptcy worthwhile.

- ✓ I know your rights and will protect them to the legal limit.

CHAPTER 7

Tax Resolutions—Better than
New Year's Resolutions

My client Ann was a widow who took a lump-sum payment from her husband's individual retirement account after he died. That decision created a big tax liability for her. The distribution was taxable, because she had not yet turned fifty-nine-and-a-half. What's more, she went from working part time to full time that same year, pushing her into a higher tax bracket. It was not until she prepared her tax return that she realized how inadequate her withholding had been and how much she owed. It was more money than she had saved or could pay. By the time she came to me, she already had gotten a collection letter for nonpayment and had taken the initiative to contact the IRS. She felt like she had made an honest mistake because she did not understand finances, which her husband had always handled.

She explained to me that the revenue agent wanted her to sell the investments she had set aside in her own retirement account, because other than her home, those were her only assets. But again, because of her age, that sale would be penalized as a premature withdrawal, it would be taxable income, and it would force her into a higher tax bracket.

Individuals like Ann, with her limited income, are generally better off if they can avoid the expense of tax resolution representation, so I encourage them to try to settle with the IRS themselves. Ann gave it a try. She asked the IRS for an installment payment agreement, and they came back with one that had her paying $300 a month. She didn't think she could afford it. She was put in a position of being forced to choose between working more hours to pay for necessities or staying home to look after sick and dying family members.

Although Ann had temporarily found full-time work, her pay and future earnings prospects were not very substantial. She had mostly been a homemaker into her mid-fifties and was unlikely to see pay increases if she could even hold on to her full-time job.

Ultimately, I went to the IRS and argued that the facts of the case summarized above justified a lower monthly payment, which we got down to $50. Ann also did not have to sell any of her retirement assets. She was thrilled.

Surely everyone with a tax problem would like to have a strong, qualified, professional advocate. This chapter will explain what to look for in a tax representative, how to hire one, and red flags to watch out for.

WHAT'S AHEAD IN THIS CHAPTER?

- The Tax Resolution Specialist's Role
- What Good Tax Representation Looks Like
- Hiring a Tax Resolution Specialist
- Red Flags to Watch Out For
- A Few Words about Good Communication

The Tax Resolution Specialist's Role

A tax resolution specialist should be able to take an objective look at the facts in a client's case, run calculations, and envision different scenarios and options. Usually several different approaches are available, and it's up to the tax resolution specialist to ask the client, "What is it you're looking for?" But he or she should also say, "Here's what I think has the best chance of succeeding."

Without the help of a tax resolution specialist, taxpayers often fail to see available strategies and, like Ann, fall into a settlement that is more painful than an alternative possibility.

By law, if you don't want to represent yourself before the IRS, you can hire a CPA, an attorney, or an enrolled agent who is licensed by the Department of the Treasury. Enrolled agents are tax specialists. CPAs, who are licensed by their state, can be working in any type of accounting and may not specialize in taxes. There are all kinds of attorneys, but someone would generally be wise to hire a tax attorney for tax court and a criminal attorney if a tax case went to criminal court.

It's still common, unfortunately, for some people who have a relationship with a CPA or lawyer to have that friend as their representative even though the person is not a tax specialist. People also turn to bankruptcy lawyers, and neither the attorney nor the client realizes until their bankruptcy case is over that certain tax liabilities were not dischargeable in the process. The client is left with no money, no credit, and a big IRS bill. The bankruptcy attorney theoretically could have represented that taxpayer in front of the IRS first, but professionals tend to focus on what they are trained to do.

About a quarter of my workday is spent just absorbing new material, as tax law and its interpretation are constantly evolving. For example, something considered a novelty or luxury a few years ago might now be an ordinary and reasonable business expense. I keep up with the changes through formal continuing education courses and doing the research that I use in my own cases and writing. As I read the blogs in which people in my industry share experiences and new approaches, I sometimes see unfortunate evidence that lawyers and accountants are taking on cases that they're not prepared to handle. They are asking, "Hey, what should I do?" I'm thinking that they either have to give themselves a crash course, if they have the time and nerves of steel, or refer the case to someone who knows what to do. But it's a paying gig, and a lot of folks will not turn away a paying gig even if they're not qualified for it.

What Good Tax Representation Looks Like

Tax resolution is a niche service that very few people do as a full-time business. Even fewer are really good at it. Those of us who are can save you substantial grief, time, and money. We can get IRS penalties waived. We can represent you all the way through the process, all the way up to tax court if we have the credentials—which I do. Most cases never get to tax court, but if you hire a tax resolution specialist, you want somebody who can represent you through audits, appeals, and mediation if necessary, standing shoulder to shoulder with you through the whole process. You should be evaluating and reevaluating strategy together. Your representative should be explaining what is happening in a manner such that you can make well-informed decisions.

Strategy with the IRS is really important, as discussed in the previous chapter. The agency has rules and regulations, but using them in your favor is more of an art than a science. A strong analytical mind can take the rules and figure out acceptable opportunities to apply guidelines to the facts of a client's case. With the client's cooperation, we may make a detailed accounting of income, expenses, and assets to see what settlement options are available short of immediate, full payment. Getting the best possible resolution takes deep knowledge of the tax rules and taxpayer rights, the people skills to understand how IRS agents think and work, understanding what the client needs and can live with, and the ability to connect all these together. That's where the art comes in. Anybody can ask the IRS what it will accept and take what's offered, as Ann initially did. The best resolution is a compromise that satisfies both the client and the IRS, but it's the client's interests that we're trying to represent.

Hiring a Tax Resolution Specialist

Once letters start coming from the IRS, the clock is running on your taxpayer rights, and it is time to take action. As your liability amount increases, so does the likelihood of your need to hire a tax resolution specialist. Higher dollar amounts require additional reporting and documentation of finances. A settlement involving a high dollar amount will be pushed up to a higher IRS management level and will take longer, and rights for challenging liabilities are time sensitive. Missed deadlines make challenges of IRS decisions more complex and expensive.

Tax resolution is by nature time-consuming. It requires a lot of study, phone calls, e-mails, and meetings, which makes it expensive compared to tax preparation. We prepare a strategy with a client and send it to the IRS, and they can reject it. Then we have to figure out why they rejected it. If they have a proper basis for the rejection, we have to come up with another strategy or research and write a challenge to the rejection. Representatives who are in over their head might tell you, "Let's settle this. You just need to pay the money," when they really mean, "I no longer want to represent you. Your case is too much work."

What's alarming is that people are looking for shortcuts. I see companies advertising to our profession, "Quit spending ten hours on a client's case. Do it in as little as twenty minutes with our new software." That's encouraging sloppy work.

So when you look for a tax resolution specialist, you have to look past the credentials and accreditations to make sure you are hiring someone willing to do the trench work. You are looking for someone who is dedicated to the specialty and to resolving your case and whose personality is a good fit with yours. Do you want someone laid-back, as many accountants tend to be, or are you more comfortable with someone like me, who is hard-charging? You may be working together for several years. Tax preparation accountants and tax lawyers who take your case to fill in a lull in their practices may be too busy when you need them.

I feel strongly that I have to have good communication, mutual respect, and a good personality match with my clients. We can both make minor adjustments to each other's preferences (for example, do we communicate by phone or e-mail?), but sometimes you find people you just can't work with. At that point, I refer them to a colleague who would be a better personality match to work alongside them throughout the case.

Red Flags to Watch Out For

In most industries, businesses look for ways to scale up to become more profitable. The way this plays out in tax resolution is that larger firms bring in salespeople who are not tax specialists but professional closers. Their job is to get you to sign an engagement letter and turn over your credit card. At that point, the salesperson disappears, and you may be turned over to a resolution assistant who, again, is not licensed to represent you but gathers all your information. Being handed off to a succession of people rather than given a professional representative for the duration of the resolution is a red flag for me. Such people might not be there in six months, but your tax problem will still be there.

Obviously it costs less to hire assistants than professionals, and that's how these companies can grow, resulting in a couple of large national corporations and several large regional companies doing tax resolution. I believe tax resolution is a very personal business and that it is conducted best by a small business. In the larger companies, the professionals too often just sign off on the work when it's finished by someone else. If you are not connecting with a professional who's going to work with you long-term, it's probably best to keep looking.

The big tax resolution companies will dispute my contention that their staff turnover hurts clients. They'll argue that their size allows them to train their staff well in-house and employ their own lawyers to seamlessly take over cases that need to go to tax court or lead to criminal charges. They'll point with pride to employees who worked their way up from salesperson to assistant and went on to become very good licensed professionals. On the other hand, some of the biggest companies have been shut down because of bad behavior that gave the whole industry a black eye. They took the clients' fees, failed to resolve the case, and then blamed the clients for not cooperating.

Some companies that advertise on radio and television are not even in the tax resolution business themselves. Instead, they aggregate sales leads and sell them to a tax resolution company at a good price. That middleman cost is then passed on to the client's bill from the tax resolution company. The people who answer phone lines from these advertisements may sound sweet, but callers should be wary. Watch out for promises that guarantee an outcome with the IRS, such as an offer in compromise for pennies on the dollar. That's not realistic. Beware the advertisement that promises you will be represented by an ex-IRS agent who has an inside track on settling IRS accounts more favorably.

A Few Words about Good Communication

In my small office, I create a personal, warm environment in which clients feel comfortable sharing concerns. If they call my office, they'll most likely get a familiar voice. It makes it easier for them to call, and by having a personal relationship, we can stay on top of keeping them in compliance with the IRS's demands for information and follow-up. Some people may be surprised by the small size of my practice, but I wouldn't have started my own firm if I didn't think I could do a better job for them than some big corporation.

Communication with my clients is a cornerstone to keeping them happy and engaged in this drawn-out process. I will e-mail or call clients personally, not just when I need information but also when they have questions or if they just have not heard anything for a while. The IRS moves slowly at times, and staying in touch with clients reassures them I haven't forgotten them—even if it feels like the IRS has.

🏛

We've covered what tax resolution specialists do, when and how to hire one, and what to expect and watch out for. The next chapter focuses on who the clients are in this business and how they got into tax trouble.

TAKE ACTION!

- ✓ The best resolution is a compromise that satisfies both the client and the IRS, but it's the client's interests that we're trying to represent.

- ✓ Tax resolution is a niche service that very few people do as a full-time business. Even fewer are really good at it. An enrolled agent who specializes is a very good option. CPAs and tax attorneys are also options.

- ✓ Look for someone who is dedicated to the specialty and to resolving your case and whose personality is a good fit with yours.

- ✓ Communication with my clients is a cornerstone to keeping them happy and engaged in this drawn-out process.

PART III
Getting Help

CHAPTER 8

When You Know You're Not Going to Fix the Problem Yourself

I represented a man I'll call "Cas" who had operated a business in the United States under the belief that as a citizen of the Netherlands, he didn't have to pay US taxes. The people served by his business also were Dutch citizens, so he decided not to charge them the sales tax required by American state and local laws. And since Cas was not planning to file US tax returns, he didn't issue any W-2 or 1099 tax statements showing his payments to employees and contractors. Cas got away with hiding all these transactions for a while, but the IRS eventually caught up with him, and his state and county tax authorities were also on his trail. I got involved then and quickly saw I was in for quite a task.

I asked to see his records, and Cas took me to a closet. He opened the door, and I was shocked at what I saw. Cas had boxes of papers scattered in no particular order, as if they had just been tossed in. His financial reports had been generated using accounting software that he no longer had, and he kept no electronic backup copies of the files.

It took some work, but using the paper files and established sources to determine standard income and expenses in his industry, we were able to generate estimates that would be acceptable to the IRS. Still, it was not clear whether his business could survive. Cas was located in a state where tax authorities, unwilling to work with estimates, were threatening to seize all of his business assets. While we were negotiating with the IRS and the state authorities, county officials surprised us by seizing the business's bank account without warning.

Cas was essentially put out of business, but a company I knew agreed to provide third-party financing so we could reopen his business—in a different county—and pay off his tax debts. Cas never really changed his attitude toward paying taxes, but at least we kept him from going to jail and saved probably a half-dozen jobs associated with his business.

I mentioned earlier that I don't work with tax protesters who make indefensible arguments about the government not having authority to levy taxes. I was able to work with Cas because there was a certain level of cooperation keeping his situation from becoming a criminal case. Cas followed the advice from his attorney and me to not openly discuss his opinions about taxes and let us talk to the authorities. Cas had a stand-up fellow working for him as the number-two manager of his company who acted as my intermediary when needed. I also met Cas's wife, who did not share her husband's attitude toward taxes. She would say to him, "Just pay the taxes so that we can go on back into our business and carry on." Cas was fortunate to have that kind of personal support, along with his own strong determination to keep his business alive. Many people who need professional tax representation have unfortunate habits or self-defeating behaviors that you'll read about in this chapter.

WHAT'S AHEAD IN THIS CHAPTER?

- What My Clients Have in Common
- The Cost of Procrastination
- Going in Unexpected Directions

What My Clients Have in Common

Most of my clients have other issues in their lives besides taxes. Some are motivated to resolve IRS collection action against them in order to prevent harm to a spouse or children. Some want to clear their cases to begin a new life with that special someone. Some, like Cas, have done business a certain way and gotten away with it, so they don't want to change. Business owners are often strong-willed people who only reluctantly let a tax resolution specialist take the lead in guiding them out of their troubles.

But most of the people I work with have something else in their lives that is devastating (besides taxes). It may be divorce, illness, business changes, or alcohol or drug abuse. Usually they come to me only after the IRS has them cornered, but occasionally they initiate the resolution effort themselves, because something in their lives has happened that makes them want to change. Even in those cases, they still need a lot of support just to stay focused on a process that takes months or years. Sometimes if things don't go fast enough, clients will contact the IRS themselves, demanding to know, "Why is this taking so long?" That kind of confrontation can undermine the image of cooperativeness that I have been presenting to the IRS on their behalf.

Working with clients who are unable to put roots down and who move around a lot is complicated. They just disappear off the radar. I need them to help me get access to documents that I can't get on my own and to be responsible enough to meet deadlines. Some clients are paralyzed by the guilt they feel about getting themselves into trouble. Sometimes I have to push clients, calling once or twice a week to check on their progress. This follow-up keeps them on track, and clients appreciate knowing that someone cares about them.

The Cost of Procrastination

Most people in tax trouble, including the people who get their companies in trouble, are procrastinators. Delays lead to penalties and interest, and then interest on the unpaid penalties just keeps the cost growing and growing. As time ticks on, the taxpayer loses some rights for appeals or certain solutions that could lower the eventual toll. As of 2017, the IRS has begun turning delinquent cases over to private collection agencies. Paying those agencies their cut increases the costs.

In addition to monetary costs, there is reputational damage. If someone has a sensitive position within a company, especially involving security clearance, and his or her wages are garnished or bank account seized, that job can be at risk. I saw a case involving a top executive of a nonprofit corporation. He personally had a huge state tax bill at the same time he was negotiating with the state to reduce a fine against his company. His bosses found out about this glaring credibility issue, and it was amazing how fast money was found somewhere to pay off his personal tax bill.

When a company owes $50,000 or more to the federal government, the IRS can have the Department of State revoke the passports of responsible executives. Imagine having that happen just before an important business trip overseas. We've previously covered how seriously the IRS takes business officers' responsibility over what the agency calls *trust fund taxes*—money withheld from employees' wages (income tax, Social Security, and Medicare taxes) by an employer and held in trust until paid to the Treasury. The next chapter explains how we handle those collection actions. We act swiftly, because when a business owner or responsible employee is implicated in nonpayment of trust fund taxes, the IRS Criminal Division can send agents to arrest that person. Imagine a family sitting down to dinner and agents leading Daddy or Mommy out of the house in handcuffs in front of the children.

Going in Unexpected Directions

As a tax resolution specialist, I know what courses of action are most likely to be successful for my clients. I analyze the individual situation, lay out the options, and find out what my clients want to accomplish. As we work through planning a strategy, we make decisions based on IRS programs they may be eligible for as well as on their personal circumstances. Clients may be able to put money into home repairs or life insurance, shielding funds that otherwise would be seized by the IRS.

We may have to address behavioral issues that are causing the tax problems, or correct problems in the business operations. With Cas, for example, I had to sit down with his number-two manager and come up with a very simplified, spreadsheet-driven, record-keeping process that he and his employees could handle. With contractor clients, I help them set up quarterly or monthly payment systems to stay ahead of their taxes.

I've recounted already how I connected clients with specialized lenders who front money to pay for an offer in compromise. More often, I am a source of emotional reassurance and act as my client's voice in talking with the IRS, to keep the client from being grilled by an overzealous agent. I protect my clients from agents who sometimes forget about taxpayers' rights. It's my job to not let my clients talk to the IRS (unless they have been issued a summons) and to be vigilant for signs a case is turning criminal. Given that dealing with tax troubles is so scary and difficult, being a caring voice and offering encouragement helps keep the client from giving up and walking away. I have to help clients accept that they are in a drawn-out struggle that may take a year to solve and require continued compliance.

Any settlement with the IRS includes a requirement that the taxpayer stay compliant in filing tax returns and making all required payments. The IRS monitors compliance, usually for five years, and maintains the option to terminate the agreement and pursue the original collection action. I offer a service in which I continue to obtain the taxpayer's IRS transcripts for those ensuing years, watching for any signs of trouble, such as late tax payments or skipped tax returns. If I spot a lapse, I warn the client and offer guidance on how to stay within the terms of the agreement with the IRS.

Battling the IRS takes a toll emotionally and requires patience and compromise. The follow-up plan I offer as a backstop for clients' continued compliance is a moral imperative for me, because I don't want to see them go through the collection and resolution process again. The second time will be more difficult and expensive.

Knowing that clients are likely to falter, I should be there to make sure they don't. I all but insist they contract with me for compliance follow-up, because it is a small price to pay to avoid falling off the rails and ending up right back where they started.

An effective tax resolution specialist must recognize and deal with the many permutations of unfortunate or dysfunctional personal and business circumstances that lead to tax problems. You've seen in this chapter how taxpayer procrastination is the most common factor in tax issues and is terribly costly to people and businesses, in both money and reputation. The next chapter addresses concerns about a trust fund recovery investigation, which can come as a surprise to more people and companies than you might expect.

TAKE ACTION!

- ✓ Most of my clients have other issues going on in their lives besides taxes—and I can help.

- ✓ Your delays lead to penalties and interest, and then interest on the unpaid penalties just keeps the cost growing and growing. As time ticks on, the taxpayer loses some rights for appeals or certain solutions that could lower the eventual toll.

- ✓ Any settlement with the IRS includes a requirement that the taxpayer stay compliant in filing tax returns and making all required payments for five years. Failure will violate the agreement and might lead to renewed collection by the IRS.

- ✓ The follow-up plan I offer as a backstop for clients' continued compliance is a moral imperative for me, because I don't want to see my clients go through the collection and resolution process again.

CHAPTER 9

Trust Fund Penalties Require Professional Help

In this chapter we return to a subject that, as I made clear in Part I, is big trouble and must be avoided by employers: mishandling the payroll taxes that the IRS calls *trust fund taxes*. The **trust fund recovery penalty** (TFRP) trips up enough companies that it is becoming a focus of my practice. I'll explain the process in detail, starting with a true story using pseudonyms to protect client confidentiality.

Don contacted me after the IRS informed him that he had a TFRP tax debt of about $263,000, which was a huge surprise to him. Don's job at a payroll processing company was to prepare payments, including tax payment checks, to be signed by Max, the majority owner of the company. The corporate payroll tax amount was calculated not by Don but by a tax preparer, and once Max signed off on the payments, they were sent by Max's administrative assistant.

Don started noticing during his bank account reconciliations that the tax payment checks were not being cashed. He contacted the IRS and asked why his company's checks had not been applied to its tax bills. He offered to reissue any lost checks. It turned out that Max had held off sending the checks, instead withdrawing the money from the bank to temporarily cover some personal debts. He kept this decision to himself, because his intention was to catch up with the tax payments as soon as possible. But what happened, as in so many such cases, was that his financial problems didn't go away. They just grew.

You may be wondering how the IRS could possibly have decided to hold Don personally liable for all the corporate payroll taxes. Don had been with the company since it began and went from being a valuable employee to becoming a minority owner. The IRS' position was that Don was a company officer, the person responsible for preparing payments, and while the IRS was not being paid, Don was writing checks to other vendors. Eventually we were able to convince the IRS that Max should be held solely responsible, because his interception of the payments was like embezzlement, making Don the victim, not a culprit. (Max was not actually charged with embezzlement, because he confessed what he had done and settled the case).

The story shows how the IRS typically acts in TFRP cases: by casting a wide net to go fishing for someone to take responsibility for the liability. The IRS does not first investigate the facts and circumstances to determine who is responsible. Like electricity, the IRS takes the path of least resistance. Any person with significant financial authority in the company or the power to direct the payment of taxes or choose which bills are paid and in what order can be a responsible person. But that statement requires further explanation, which you'll find below.

WHAT'S AHEAD IN THIS CHAPTER?

- "Trust Fund Recovery Penalty" Is Confusing
- Pinning Responsibility
- The In-Person Interview
- Resolving a Case without an Interview
- Challenging a Trust Fund Penalty
- How Trust Fund Cases Vary
- Signs of a Criminal Case
- Having a Defensible Position

"Trust Fund Recovery Penalty" Is Confusing

An employer gets into the position of handling the government's money as soon as the company issues a paycheck that contains payroll tax deductions. If employees are paid weekly and the tax payments are remitted to the IRS quarterly, a significant amount of money could be held in trust by the employer in the interim. Companies, or their employees who handle that money, are strictly acting as a responsible fiduciary to protect those funds until they can be turned over to the rightful owner: the US Treasury. It is not their option to borrow it or to use it, but only to protect it, preferably in a separate account.

"Borrowing" the money the IRS calls trust fund taxes is more like robbing a bank than like taking a bank loan. That's a simple concept, but the underlying law is much more complicated, because it has to deal with the many circumstances and schemes that have occurred in which people have misappropriated trust fund taxes.

Tax law sets two requirements to determine TFRP liability: Responsibility and willfulness both must be established for a person to be liable. It is possible for a person to be responsible but not willful, or the other way around. The IRS may assess anyone and everyone who is responsible and willful for unpaid trust fund taxes during the quarter they are due if those taxes cannot be immediately collected from the business. TFRP contains the word "penalty," but that's misleading—it is an assessment of tax owed, not an *addition* to tax.

The TFRP equals the amount of tax evaded, not collected, or not accounted for and paid over. Normally, the amount of the TFRP equals withheld income taxes plus one-half of the Social Security tax liability. Federal unemployment taxes and penalties or interest assessed against the employer are not included. The IRS can consider imposing penalties or bringing a criminal case if circumstances warrant, but it does not automatically add on the 20 percent accuracy-related penalty or the 75 percent civil fraud penalty faced by those who fail to pay income taxes.[10]

Pinning Responsibility

The responsible person who receives a TFRP assessment can be an officer, employee, director, or shareholder of a company; one partner in a partnership; an employee in a sole proprietorship; or even an outside entity that provides the company money knowing that it will be used to pay employees but not their payroll taxes. In the story at

---

10 Internal Revenue Code § 6672(a).

the beginning of the chapter, responsibility was pinned at first on Don.

The Internal Revenue Manual makes clear that a clerk who is supervised by someone else and does not have the authority to make independent decisions will not be deemed responsible, but there is no absolute, conclusive rule for pinning responsibility. IRS agents will look at who signs checks and decides in what order the vendors are paid, but the mere authority to sign checks does not establish responsibility.

As defined by the Internal Revenue Manual, *willful* means "intentional, deliberate, voluntary, reckless, knowing, as opposed to accidental." The IRS must prove that the responsible person was aware of, or should have been aware of, the outstanding tax liability but intentionally disregarded the law or was plainly indifferent to its requirements. A responsible person's failure to review or correct this after being informed that withholding taxes that have not been paid satisfies the willfulness element. The IRS manual adds that "no evil intent or bad motive is required."[11]

A court case held that willfulness means that the act of non-payment was voluntarily, consciously, and intentionally done or omitted. A willful failure results when a responsible person is aware of the unpaid trust fund taxes but consciously pays the amount to others (Barnett v. IRS, 1993).

The In-Person Interview

The IRS Collection Division will insist that the target of a TFRP investigation submit to an in-person question and answer session in which the revenue officer completes IRS Form 4180, a report

11 Internal Revenue Manual 5.7.3.3.2

summing up the interview. The targeted individual is told to sign the form, attesting to it being factual and accurate. I advise you not to appear before the IRS to provide testimony or answer questions. Hire a qualified tax resolution expert to do your talking for you.

Often, revenue officers have already decided that the investigation target is personally liable, and the in-person interview is aimed at collecting evidence of liability based on answers to IRS trick questions. Having that evidence on file in a signed form allows the revenue officer to move on to the next step: preparing an internal IRS recommendation for the TFRP. Once a manager approves the recommendation, the IRS can issue an assessment, which you know from previous chapters can lead to liens and seizure of your property.

The IRS has good reason to be very aggressive in collecting trust fund taxes, if you think about it from the agency's perspective. In deducting the money from the employee paycheck, the employer made a written promise to pay those taxes to the US Treasury. When payroll tax deposits are missed, the government loses that revenue twice. First, it doesn't get the taxes. And second, the IRS has to credit employees' accounts with tax payments their employers were required to make. Remember, tax money's final destination is not the IRS, but the US Treasury, which uses it to pay its obligations, including Social Security, Medicare, and tax refunds. Payroll taxes must be collected because they are the major funding source, on a daily basis, for US government operations.

If you are responsible for willfully failing to pay these payroll taxes, you must accept the fact that you will be held accountable and move on to planning a strategy to resolve that liability. Your professional tax representative will help figure out the best way to pay the debt, which may involve an offer in compromise or installment agreement, and to avoid criminal prosecution. However, if you do not think you should be held responsible, then definitely hire an enrolled agent, a CPA with knowledge in this area, or a tax attorney.

When a taxpayer shows up for a 4180 interview without understanding the importance of the procedure, the results can be disastrous. The meeting may appear informal, but it can have long-lasting and far-reaching ramifications.

Resolving a Case without an Interview

There are four ways to end a TFRP investigation without having to submit to an interview:

1. Agree to the TFRP and cancel the interview—Let's say we determine that, ultimately, you failed to see to it that the taxes were paid, which will make you personally liable for the debt. The revenue officer has discretion to end your investigation once you have notified the IRS that you are in agreement.

2. Direct-debit streamlined installment agreement—If the employment tax liability is under $25,000 and the business can pay it back within twenty-four months by direct debit out of its bank account, the revenue officer may end the investigation.

3. Inability to pay—Even if you are liable for the TFRP, proving to the IRS that you could never pay it is a way to end the investigation. In practice, revenue agents often go ahead with the assessment anyway by being tough in how they interpret the standard of whether the debt could ever be collected.

4. Statute of limitations—The IRS has three years to do its trust fund investigation and interview you.[12]

12 Internal Revenue Manual 5.19.14.1.5 (January 13, 2016).

The IRS sends a notice to any person determined to be responsible who willfully did not pay the payroll taxes. This notice will, with some exceptions, be issued at least sixty days prior to issuing a demand for remittance of the TFRP. The taxpayer does have some rights to appeal, but running out the clock is not a viable strategy, especially if colleagues already have lawyered up and are deflecting blame from themselves. If you anticipate getting a TFRP assessment or have been assessed, contact a qualified professional to avoid further action by the collection arm of the IRS. Responding properly can prevent or mitigate civil or criminal penalties. Time is not on your side.

Challenging a Trust Fund Penalty

I have seen several different types of situations in which the IRS assessed a TFRP when it should not have. Sometimes the circumstances and facts of the case were just not that clear. There may have been a dispute in ownership and responsibilities, or documentation of responsibilities was lax, so an employee inaccurately appeared to be in control of how and if payroll tax deposits were made. Perhaps an accounting department employee had the authority to sign checks but had no actual control over company finances.

Other erroneous TFRPs I've seen stemmed from the aggressiveness of the IRS and/or a lack of professional representation:

- A revenue officer wanting to name as many people as possible as targets

- A taxpayer signing the agreement form just to appease the revenue officer

- Making a scapegoat out of a non-responsible party who didn't know how to fight back

To challenge the TFRP, we need to show that you were not responsible or willful—one or the other. To win on the responsibility defense, we must prove to the IRS that you did not have control over the company's decision-making process and finances. The willfulness defense includes showing a lack of knowledge about what's happening in the business regarding the payment of the employment taxes. To succeed, it is not enough to simply not have known about the nonpayment. You must prove you could not have known payroll taxes were not being paid.

Business owners these days face countless demands on their time and resources. However, anyone in a position to be considered responsible for making payroll tax payments cannot afford to let those issues go unattended. I want to emphasize again that you can be responsible and therefore liable even if you have no knowledge that the IRS is not being paid. In a business with multiple owners, officers, and check signers, they all may draw a penalty assessment. These people generally respond by protecting themselves and doing their best to point the IRS toward someone else. Depending on the facts, circumstantial nuances, and legal maneuvering, one responsible person may get stuck paying while a savvy participant escapes without paying anything.

How Trust Fund Cases Vary

I have described a few cases in which relatively small businesses purposely held on to trust fund taxes in a misguided effort to solve cash-flow problems. That is a form of pyramiding, which can also involve companies playing an intentional shell game in which they keep changing the names and ownership, each time paying just enough taxes to keep going. TFRP cases also come in other forms of varying complexity and criminality:

Employment leasing—It is legal for a business to contract out personnel administration and payroll to another company, including offshore employee leasing. It becomes a TFRP case if that outside company dissolves, leaving payroll taxes unpaid.

Fraudulent payroll returns/no returns—An employer might purposely understate the amount of wages on which taxes are owed in order to cheat on payroll taxes. A dishonest corporate finance employee might embezzle the withheld taxes, file no returns, and remain unsuspected by senior management until it is too late. The IRS maintains a whistleblower program to encourage employees to report these abuses.

Cash payment—The IRS website warns, "Paying employees, whole or partially, in cash is a common method of evading income and employment taxes resulting in lost tax revenue to the government and the loss or reduction of future Social Security or Medicare benefits for the employee." Companies that mostly receive and pay cash are hard for the IRS to investigate, because auditing is records-dependent. But agents are trained to find clues, such as if a company's activities require six workers, but records show payment for only two workers.

Executive compensation disguised as corporation distribution—The distributions are not usually subject to payroll tax.

Worker status classification schemes—Businesses of all sizes may run into payroll tax problems by intentionally or unintentionally misclassifying employees as independent contractors. The practice becomes rampant in some industries until there is a crackdown, and then it crops up in different industries.

 ## Melissa's Story

One of my colleagues was contacted by the parents of a teenaged high school graduate who had gotten her first job as a receptionist in a real estate office. The sales people in the office were all independent contractors, so they classified this teenager, whom I'll call "Melissa," the same way. She didn't understand that the company was not only avoiding paying her any benefits but also not deducting any taxes, including the Social Security and Medicare payroll taxes, from her paycheck. It was not until the next year at tax filing time that Melissa discovered she owed several thousand dollars in taxes.

That situation raises the question, "Whose responsibility is it here?" The employer wanted to call Melissa an independent contractor, but by law she was clearly an employee, working full time in an office under close supervision and using company equipment. The company was skirting the law to save money.

After the company issued Melissa a Form 1099 showing her income reported to the IRS, my colleague advised her to file a Form SS-8, which is a request for the IRS to review the facts of her employment situation and determine whether or not she's an employee or an independent contractor. Once the IRS rules that she is an employee, the company then becomes responsible for paying her back taxes. I was told that Melissa's reaction to the advice was, "If I do that, they're going to fire me." In fact, the company will quite likely react by coincidentally discovering it no longer can afford a receptionist, eliminating her job. At that point, Melissa can consult an attorney about suing for wrongful dismissal or (more likely, as she is a teenager) just move on with her life.

The alternative to trying to hold the company responsible was for her parents to help her pay the taxes. But I agree with my colleague's advice to try to make the company do the right thing.

Signs of a Criminal Case

An important step often overlooked by tax resolution specialists is early identification of potential criminal liability. The IRS Criminal Investigation division investigates suspected lawbreakers to promote taxpayer compliance, and while it recommends prosecution of only a few thousand cases a year, most of those cases result in convictions, so it's important to take the appropriate steps to protect the client from prosecution as soon as possible.

A criminal case usually begins with a routine audit. IRS office and field employees are trained to identify indicators of potential fraud. If they see those badges of fraud (described in chapter 4), they refer the case to Criminal Investigation. After IRS investigators determine that a crime has been committed, they refer the case to the Justice Department for evaluation and possible prosecution.

Let's focus on the early elements of the process. The frontline revenue agents may be artful at spotting taxpayers who are excessively nervous and uncooperative, but using those powers of observation to identify criminal activity is not an exact science. The revenue agents will attempt to gather additional information beyond the badges of fraud before referring a case to Criminal Investigation. Requests for information that go beyond what would ordinarily be required to conclude an examination are a warning sign that a criminal investigation might be coming. It also may already be underway, as the IRS does not have to disclose if it is simultaneously conducting civil and criminal investigations. The IRS rules forbid lying to or misleading the taxpayer on any important issue, but an agent does not have to answer a question about an investigation, even if asked directly by a professional taxpayer representative.

One or more Criminal Investigation agents may work a case, possibly with personnel from other federal agencies, primarily the FBI, Drug Enforcement Administration, and the Bureau of Alcohol, Tobacco, Firearms, and Explosives. Their job is preparing a case for prosecution, for which they need more than vague "badges of fraud."

Under current law, a willful failure to pay over or collect tax is a felony punishable by up to a $10,000 fine, five years in prison, or both. The IRS reserves criminal charges for the most outrageous cases, such as where a business owner diverted the money for his or her personal use, rather than situations where an owner or other responsible person in a business that was facing hard times used the money to pay other creditors in a misguided attempt to keep the business afloat.

As soon as we believe a case has turned into a criminal investigation, the taxpayer should immediately stop talking to the IRS and hire an attorney experienced in criminal tax cases. Communications with the attorney provide the confidentiality protection of attorney-client privilege. An attorney working on a criminal case can extend that privilege to a federally licensed tax representative, such as me, through what is called a **Kovel agreement**.

Note this important distinction: The power of attorney that a taxpayer gives to a CPA or enrolled agent by signing Form 2848 (Power of Attorney and Declaration of Representative) does *not* provide attorney-client protection. So if my client's case "turns criminal," the client should revoke the Form 2848 and engage a criminal attorney instead. Otherwise, any admissions I make to the IRS would be treated as though the taxpayer had made the statements. Most taxpayers who successfully defend against a criminal tax case never speak, or have only limited conversation, with IRS agents, letting their attorneys do the talking.

Having a Defensible Position

New schemes are always emerging to circumvent payroll tax obligations. As I write this book, a new scheme getting the attention of IRS enforcement involves workers being hired as independent contractors and then paid to rent their equipment and tools back to the company. So, what's really wages or income instead shows up as a rental fee. Companies will try new schemes like that until the IRS rules them out.

The "sharing economy" business model promoted by technology companies has created its share of work for the IRS. For example, ride-hailing services such as Uber and Lyft employ a lot of independent contractors, and the IRS must determine whether that employment classification is legitimate as the norm in a new industry or should be circumvented with new regulations. In previous years, well-known corporations that deliver packages and develop software got hit with back taxes and paid settlements over misclassifying contract employees.

The IRS says that if 25 percent of your industry follows the practice of calling a certain type of employee an independent contractor, it's a defensible position. You may follow that practice and have the IRS rule against you, but you're not going to be hit with major fines and interest. Cases are complex, unique, and fact-driven, so when businesses are in a bad economy or an industry with tight profit margins, they are tempted to try any scheme that seems defensible.

Just remember that when the IRS decides there has been responsible and willful nonpayment of payroll taxes, revenue agents will cast a wide net to pin the liability on someone. An innocent person may be targeted and forced to spend time and money avoiding potential criminal prosecution. The next chapter looks at how injustices can happen and what we do when a taxpayer in trouble encounters hardball tactics instead of fair treatment.

TAKE ACTION!

- ✓ Payroll taxes must be collected because they are the major funding source, on a daily basis, for US government operations.

- ✓ In trust fund cases, responsibility and willfulness both must be established for a person to be liable.

- ✓ The taxpayer does have some rights to appeal, but running out the clock is not a viable strategy, especially if colleagues already have lawyered up and are deflecting blame from themselves.

- ✓ If a case becomes criminal, a tax representative can work with an attorney through a Kovel agreement, which extends attorney-client privilege to the tax rep.

CHAPTER 10

Being Treated Like a Criminal

One of my favorite tax resolution stories didn't involve me, but I want to tell it because it starts off really bad and has a happy ending. It involves a man who went to prison for a series of crimes. While he was incarcerated, he was transformed by finding Jesus. After embracing Christianity and being saved, his good behavior led to early release. He had decided in prison that he would start a church as soon as he was free, and he did so in a small storefront. Slowly the church grew, and like all pastors, he had to file his personal income tax return and an informational tax return for the church to support its nonprofit status. The IRS challenged the legitimacy of his church, assuming it was a ploy by an ex-convict to avoid taxes.

The pastor tried to explain that he had been saved and his life was different now, but the IRS didn't buy it. The pastor contacted a tax resolution specialist for help. Although he didn't have enough money to mount a vigorous defense, the pastor hoped my colleague, Ben, would give him some guidance on how to persuade the IRS that his church was legitimate. Ben, who happens to be Jewish, was skeptical at first but talked with the pastor long enough, in multiple conversations, to decide he was on the level about devoting his life to Christian service. Ben took on the case pro bono and met with the IRS agent handling the case. The agent just kind of looked at him in disbelief that he would be representing an ex-con who had such a bad history.

But Ben persisted, going back and forth with the agent for nearly two years, presenting evidence that a transformation had occurred in his client. In the end, the IRS agent was convinced and closed the case in favor of the pastor.

An IRS agent looks for badges of fraud to cast doubt on a church's legitimacy, unlike in a criminal case where investigators hope "smoking gun" evidence will prove guilt beyond a reasonable doubt. The standard of evidence to prove or disprove the legitimacy of a church is not that clear-cut, so a case like this ex-convict's comes down to credibility, which no doubt was helped by the willingness of the tax resolution specialist to risk his reputation and help argue the case pro bono.

WHAT'S AHEAD IN THIS CHAPTER?

- Hardball IRS Tactics
- Private Collection Agencies
- How to Avoid the Hammer

Hardball IRS Tactics

Our tax system is built on voluntary compliance. It doesn't have the enforcement resources to catch everyone who might want to misbehave. But as we'll see in this chapter, the IRS has ways to encourage voluntary compliance through harsh treatment of those it thinks are failing to comply, including recommending a small number of cases for criminal investigation. These cases almost always result in convictions, because IRS agents and the agency's lawyers work together to pick their cases carefully and try to make examples out of these people.

More typically, the IRS determines that a liability exists and puts a lien on all of the taxpayer's property. This action intentionally creates a hardship for the taxpayer, notably a drop in credit scores and an inability to borrow money. Restricting the taxpayer's cash flow, especially if it is a business, makes it harder to raise the funds to pay off the tax liability or even to hire a professional to resolve the tax issue. But if the taxpayer does not act quickly, assets can be seized and sold for discounted values, adding to the financial hardship.

For example, if the IRS seizes a piece of equipment worth $100,000, agency rules consider it reasonable to sell it for at least 80 percent of that value. If the asset is not easy to sell, the IRS could end up taking even less money. If the sale proceeds are $60,000, the business gets that amount applied to its tax bill, regardless of the asset's original value. That's a bad outcome by any measure and is the kind of enforcement that often results in businesses shutting down.

With individual taxpayers, IRS rules do not allow the agency to seize and sell someone's home or car or to question lifestyle choices that went into those purchases. But in considering an offer in compromise, agents do pressure taxpayers to lower their expenses, so they will question why someone can't trade down to a smaller house, rent a less expensive apartment, or trade in a luxury car for a cheaper mode of transport. An offer may be denied if expenses exceed national, state, and local guidelines the IRS uses. For example, a taxpayer is allowed a certain amount for purchase and upkeep of a car. The IRS could question why the taxpayer recently bought a luxury car and whether it was a strategy to convert assets into something shielded from seizure. The taxpayer would have to justify the purchase.

Taxpayers who have a lot of debt may be forced to file for bankruptcy protection from creditors because of hardball IRS collection tactics. Not all tax liabilities are dischargeable in bankruptcy, as we explained in chapter 6 of this book, so tax representatives work with bankruptcy attorneys to determine the tax liability after bankruptcy. Taxes must be paid ahead of any discretionary expenses, so family members must be warned not to expect any "extras." And as we saw in chapter 4, college tuition and wedding expenses are among those extras that the IRS allows only after the taxes are paid.

Essentially, when the IRS sees a taxpayer falling behind on payments, it takes out a hammer to fix the problem. The collection process does not start by trying to sort out those with criminal intent from those who are merely suffering financial misfortune. Businesses are particularly susceptible to the hardball tactics for three reasons:

1. There are not many limits to business property the IRS can seize. Generally, the IRS must leave a business with about $5,000 in assets, under current guidelines, but that's not enough to keep any substantial company from being effectively shut down.

2. If the IRS is trying to collect trust fund penalties, it can pursue any individual who had any influence in collecting

those payroll taxes. The finger-pointing among corporate officers can devastate a business.

3.   A tax lien gives businesses a hard time getting credit. Many businesses, especially the smaller ones, rely on credit lines because their revenues ebb and flow while their expenses remain constant, as they have to pay employees and utilities year-round.

Private Collection Agencies

The IRS has limited time and money to pursue collections, and starting in 2017 it began turning some cases over to private collection agencies. Usually these are older cases running up against the statute of limitations. The IRS had tested private debt collection in the past without much success, but in 2015 Congress passed a law that tightened the IRS budget and required the agency to use private collection agencies in a program that is likely to expand. Some states also use private debt collectors.

One concern is that the private companies will be less respectful of taxpayer rights than the IRS, which is answerable to Congress. The collection agencies can hire whomever they want, and their bottom line is based on how much they can collect. If they get caught misbehaving, all they have to do is ask for forgiveness from IRS management. Another concern is that the private collection agencies blur the line separating IRS agents from scam artists who pretend to be tax collectors.

How to Avoid the Hammer

Some of us would like to see the IRS take a gentler approach and become less of an existential threat and more of a coach to taxpayers who need some help getting back into compliance. For now, my advice to those seeking to make the IRS an ally is to avoid delay and come in to the IRS voluntarily with their properly prepared solutions. The success of this approach depends on the circumstances, as we have seen in the stories in this book—the innocent spouse, the widow with the temporary job, and the businesspeople targeted by an IRS that has made trust fund collection a high priority. For those trust fund cases and others involving a large amount of money, my advice is to call me or another tax resolution professional immediately.

Occasionally, the IRS announces a limited program to collect tax on previously undeclared income from various sources, with the promise that the taxpayers who come forward will not be prosecuted. It's typically a very short window of opportunity and includes partial clemency on interest and penalties. The goal of such amnesty programs is to collect as much revenue as possible in a short period of time. The last such program I recall was in 2012–14 and involved foreign bank account reporting. The IRS got offshore institutions to provide data on formerly secret accounts and then gave the account holders a chance to file returns without interest and penalties.

Once it acts to collect back taxes, the IRS has a certain amount of time until the agency has to write the case off as a loss and remove any liens (except in cases of fraud). Agents have no patience with people who are trying to run out the clock. The agents' goal is to collect all the taxes due before the expiration date. The IRS offers a Fresh Start Program that is a packaged version of the installment agreements we discussed in chapters 3 and 5. The program can work for taxpayers capable of paying their full liability, including interest and penalties, in installments by the expiration date. For taxpayers who cannot pay the full amount, the program allows the IRS the option to collect as much of the tax as possible. The program raises the threshold of tax liability before the IRS will issue a tax lien, but the IRS retains the option to ignore that provision. The IRS doesn't let go of the hammer easily.

We've seen in this chapter that the IRS has some discretion to close a collection case or help a taxpayer get into compliance, but hardball tactics are the agency's standard operating procedure. When the IRS gets out the hammer, the best protection for a taxpayer is proper professional representation, which the next chapter will explain how to find.

TAKE ACTION!

- ✔ For trust fund cases and other cases involving a large amount of money, my advice is to call me or another tax resolution professional immediately.

- ✔ The IRS has once again employed private collection agencies. History is littered with undesirable outcomes. Get in front of this by contacting a tax professional.

- ✔ The IRS employs a hammer to collect taxes. Tax amnesty programs are rare.

CHAPTER 11

Taxation with Proper Representation

Sometimes tax problems happen to good people who aren't doing anything wrong. Remember back in chapter 1, when I mentioned my client Gary in Indiana (yes, like the city) who operated medical clinics in several different counties? Each location was a separate entity, but his centralized accounting staff kept good records and was timely about filing federal, state, and county taxes as a private, nonprofit corporation. In fact, the business—mostly geriatric rehabilitation—paid so much tax that it was in danger of losing money. Gary eventually decided to relocate his business to another part of the country that was more tax-friendly to him. I was working as an accountant back then and helped him file the correct paperwork to officially close his business in Indiana. He even tore down one of the buildings he owned.

Then Gary started receiving letters from the Indiana Department of Revenue saying he had failed to file tax returns and that state tax collectors had gone ahead and estimated his taxes. Those estimates are always quite high, and with the added interest, penalties, and interest on unpaid penalties, my client got a whopping bill. Gary made several calls to state officials over time and was told not to worry about it and that they recognized it was an error but couldn't stop their computerized system from generating those notices. For whatever reason, however, the account was turned over to a collection company that started bothering Gary at his new business to pay Indiana $150,000 in payroll taxes, including for staff at the building that no longer existed.

I agreed to help and ran into much of the same confusion and denial as Gary did with the state agency. Officials said there was nothing they could do. When I persisted, they put me through a maze of tasks producing corporate records showing the business had shut down, but it was never enough to satisfy the state. Eventually the state announced a tax amnesty program that included contact information for someone who could make a decision on settling tax bills. Because of that program, I finally was able to get through easily to someone who made a decision to close the case. It was never clear why we couldn't reach such a person through normal channels and had to wait for the amnesty program to come along. But at least the collection letters and threats stopped, and my client could focus on his profession, which included helping people in poor, rural counties with their medical issues.

WHAT'S AHEAD IN THIS CHAPTER?

- When You Call Your Accountant

- Tax Resolution License Requirements
- Advantages of Specialization
- The Right to Representation
- Why This Niche Was Right for Me

When You Call Your Accountant

People with tax issues often turn to their accountant or lawyer for help because of the existing relationship. But there are two questions to ask first:

- Is the accountant or lawyer an enrolled agent—someone who has earned the privilege of representing taxpayers before the IRS through professional experience or by passing comprehensive examinations?

- Does the accountant or lawyer practice tax resolution enough to be up-to-date on the latest rules and best procedures?

Only an estimated 5 percent of enrolled agents do tax resolution full time. It is a small niche practice for both lawyers and accountants. CPAs, whose focus is tax preparation, are generally not prepared to handle the kinds of cases that require a tax resolution specialist but may be reluctant to say so, because they either think they can handle the work or just don't want to lose the client or the revenue.

TAX RESOLUTION LICENSE REQUIREMENTS

Certified tax resolution specialists and enrolled agents work only in tax preparation and tax resolution—truly a specialized niche. But others can offer tax resolution.

A CPA is licensed by a state board of accountancy. To earn the license, the accountant must demonstrate knowledge and competence by meeting high educational standards, passing the Uniform CPA Exam, and completing a specific amount of general accounting experience as required by the state in which the accountant wants to practice.

An enrolled agent is a person who has earned the privilege of representing taxpayers before the Internal Revenue Service, either by passing a three-part, comprehensive IRS test covering individual and business tax returns or through experience as a former IRS employee. Enrolled agent status is the highest credential the IRS awards. Individuals who obtain this elite status must adhere to ethical standards and complete seventy-two hours of continuing education courses every three years.

Enrolled agents, like attorneys and CPAs, are unrestricted as to which taxpayers they can represent, what types of tax matters they can handle, and which IRS offices they can represent clients before.

A tax resolution specialist may obtain certification and additional credentials through membership in professional associations that provide training focused not on taxes in general but specifically on dealing with the IRS.

If a tax preparer may be at fault for errors or omissions in tax preparation and is vulnerable to a lawsuit from a taxpayer, the case is generally turned over to insurance company lawyers. Their main goal is not resolving the taxpayer's case but instead minimizing the damage. If they can satisfy the client with a payment, they can head off a lawsuit that would be more costly to the insurance company and could lead to sanctions against the tax preparer, such as license suspension. But if a client comes to me and says, "My accountant has messed up my taxes, and now the IRS is saying that I owe a bunch of money," I can blame the accountant when I make the client's case with the IRS.

Accountants sometimes fool themselves into thinking tax resolution will be a good add-on to their business, but when they find out how labor-intensive it is, how many phone calls they're making, and how much documentation they are submitting over and over again, it becomes a burden. The risk is that these accountants will turn the work over to non-licensed assistants and just sign off on it, which is not the kind of representation the client deserves. The outcome of a tax case can be determined by the smallest details, which can be overlooked if a specialist is not working personally and consistently with the client. The IRS is playing to win, so we should be playing to win, too.

Advantages of Specialization

Tax resolution is not only time-consuming but also involves personal skills that are different from those typically exercised by CPAs and lawyers. The relationship between the practitioner and client must be strong enough to endure over a long period of time in which the client must avoid procrastination, be honest, and follow strict rules, which generally are not the common traits of those in tax trouble.

The tax resolution specialist also has to maintain a relationship with the IRS agent to present the client in the best light.

The niche of tax resolution takes the right kind of person who is willing and able to simultaneously be patient with the client and assertive with the IRS. Accountants tend to be detail-oriented people who enjoy working by themselves, but tax resolution is a process of negotiation—not just analysis of financial documents. There is almost a certain amount of evangelism that comes into play in making the client's case to an IRS agent.

The Right to Representation

A story making the rounds among tax resolution specialists under-lines the danger of not having vigorous representation. A woman was summoned to an IRS office to defend her position that she was the victim of identity theft. She was afraid to go by herself and hired someone to accompany her who was licensed to do so but really had no experience as a tax representative. The two of them showed up at the IRS office, which is purposely designed to be an intimidating place, even beyond its having armed agents.

The agent who greeted them told the representative, "You won't be part of this meeting," to which he properly replied by presenting a signed power of attorney to represent his client. The IRS agent did not relent, saying, "I see it. But you're not going to be in this meeting." The tax rep asked, "Have they changed the law?" And the IRS agent said, "No, they haven't changed the law. Will you please take a seat in the other room?"

After his client emerged from the meeting, the tax rep asked her, "Why didn't you say something? Why didn't you say, 'He's my representative. I'm not going to do this without him?'"

She said, "I brought you along because I was too afraid. I was afraid that if I spoke up, the IRS would come down on me hard. I brought you here to represent me." Anyone who specializes in tax resolution develops the skills to stand up for taxpayer rights and would have stopped that meeting.

Eventually, the representative got the IRS to admit the agent made a mistake, but only after being given the false excuse that the agent didn't know the representative had a signed power of attorney. A tax resolution specialist would never have let the client go into that meeting unaccompanied. We know that taxpayers have the right to retain representation, and if they give that right away, the IRS is not going to give it back to them.

Why This Niche Was Right for Me

I got into tax resolution after sixteen years of doing corporate and personal tax preparation. I had discovered over time how getting to the right person and telling the right story could solve many tax problems. Tax officials are bureaucrats who have a desk full of work they need to clear, just like corporate office workers do. For the IRS, it adds up to more than $400 billion worth of taxes due, which means there are a lot of people in need of tax resolution. I recognized that I have the skills and the interest to win tax cases, and I enjoy doing so.

Some of my clients' victories are big and easy to measure, like when I was able to reclaim a whole year's worth of employment taxes for a Kentucky business that had made a small computer programming error in its payroll system. Other times I meet with people who realize they cannot afford my services, but I explain to them how they can protect themselves and send them on their way with greater knowledge of taxpayer rights.

I've helped accountants who can't do their own taxes, believe it or not. They may have spent their careers doing other types of work, and they know better than to try to represent themselves to the IRS. The same goes for attorneys, who are susceptible to tax problems if they fail to claim all of their income. Lawyers may get paid by many individual clients who are not filing 1099 forms with the IRS to document those payments, creating a temptation for the lawyer to underreport. And like any small business, a law firm has constant expenses, but income ebbs and flows.

Some of my clients, like Gary, the medical clinic operator in Indiana, are good people who feel like they're lost in a strange land where they don't know the roads, the language, or the people. Being their guide makes me feel like I'm doing something worthwhile. Plus, I'm good at it, and I take pride in my work. It's certainly more satisfying than sitting at a desk and doing corporate taxes day after day.

Tax resolution work is not something that you can hire just any CPA or attorney, or even any enrolled agent, to do and get the best results. They'll take the work and are licensed to do it, but they're not necessarily qualified for it. If you have read this far, you have gotten to know my approach to tax resolution and my dedication to my clients. In the conclusion, I invite you to contact me if you need help from a tax resolution specialist.

TAKE ACTION!

- ✅ People with tax issues often turn to their accountant or lawyer for help because of the existing relationship, but are they an enrolled agent or a tax resolution specialist?

- The niche of tax resolution takes the right kind of person who is willing and able to simultaneously be patient with the client and assertive with the IRS. Accountants tend to be detail-oriented people who enjoy working by themselves.

- I got into tax resolution after sixteen years of doing corporate and personal tax preparation. I had discovered over time how getting to the right person and telling the right story could solve many tax problems.

CONCLUSION

New Life Tax Resolution

Although I make a living in tax resolution, I don't wish tax trouble on anyone, so the first third of this book focused on how to avoid tax problems. We talked about keeping your eye on your taxes even if you hire someone else to keep your books and prepare your returns. You can't ignore this part of your business, so you need to learn at least the basics of tax law. Hiring an outsider to periodically check your business systems for tax compliance is money well spent.

The second part of the book covered what happens to people who get into tax trouble, and the most important two words of advice were "don't delay." You have the right to representation, but you can handle a small liability by yourself. A qualified tax representative can help you find out what the IRS knows about you, plan a strategy, and help you talk to IRS agents. You may be able to approach the

IRS and arrive at a settlement you can live with. If the discussions or negotiations do not go well, you can stop at any time and get help from a tax resolution specialist, who can appeal your case to higher management levels or even all the way to tax court.

The third and final part of the book focused on the value of professional tax resolution. If you have serious problems with taxes; if the amount is substantial (over $15,000); or if you have TFRP issues; you need a professional. If you are under criminal investigation, you need professional help immediately. The IRS uses hardball tactics that can put people out of business or destroy their lives. Not everyone licensed to deal with the IRS is prepared to handle difficult tax resolution cases, but my firm is.

My firm, New Life Tax Resolution, is located in Celebration, Florida, but I can represent anybody in the fifty states, plus Puerto Rico, with federal and state tax issues.

You can find more information by visiting my website at **NewLifeTaxResolutions.com** or by calling us at 844-868-3170. We answer our own phones on weekdays, and if you mention that you read this book, you will receive a $250 discount on any representation services we perform on your behalf. Thank you.

GLOSSARY

appeal: Because people sometimes disagree on tax matters, the Service has an appeal system. Most differences can be settled within this system.

assessment: An IRS determination that a taxpayer owes a certain amount of money.

badges of fraud: Suspicious behavior, such as a taxpayer taking an unrealistically aggressive stance, refusing or failing to turn over documents, and missing appointments.

certified tax resolution specialists: The Certified Tax Resolution Specialist designation is awarded to individuals who have met the educational, experience, and examination requirements prescribed by the American Society of Tax Problem Solvers (ASTPS).

enrolled agent: A person who has earned the privilege of representing taxpayers before the Internal Revenue Service either by passing a three-part, comprehensive IRS test covering individual and business tax returns or through experience as a former IRS employee.

Freedom of Information Act (FOIA): A law granting the right to access records from the federal government. Federal agencies are required to disclose any information requested under the FOIA unless it falls under one of nine exemptions that protect interests such as personal privacy, national security, and law enforcement.

Kovel agreement: Extending attorney-client privilege of confidential communications to an accountant who is working with the attorney on a criminal case as a federally authorized tax representative. There is no accountant-client privilege outside of a Kovel agreement.

levy: An IRS levy permits the legal seizure of a taxpayer's property to satisfy a tax debt. It can take money from a bank or other financial account; seize and sell vehicle(s), real estate, and other personal property; or be attached to the taxpayer's future income.

lien: A federal tax lien is the government's legal claim against the property of a taxpayer who has neglected or failed to pay a tax debt. The lien protects the government's interest in the property, including real estate, personal property, and financial assets.

offer in compromise: A taxpayer can make an offer in compromise to settle a tax debt for less than the full amount owed. The IRS investigates the taxpayer's income, expenses, and assets, and then determines whether the taxpayer legitimately cannot pay the full tax liability.

payroll taxes: Federal income tax withholding; the FICA old-age, survivors, and disability insurance taxes, also known as Social Security taxes; and the hospital insurance tax, also known as Medicare taxes. These taxes are generally withheld by employers from employees' paychecks and are also paid by employers and contractors in their estimated tax payments.

substitute for return (SFR): When a taxpayer fails to file a return, the IRS creates one based upon estimates plus interest and penalties. The SFR usually creates a much larger tax liability than a properly prepared original return.

trust fund recovery penalty (TFRP): An IRS determination that someone personally responsible for employee payroll taxes willfully failed to properly direct the payment of those taxes and is liable for that payment plus interest.

wage garnishment: Wage garnishment, wage attachment, and wage levy are three different terms for the way officials can order employers to withhold a specific sum from an employee's wages to satisfy a tax debt or other legal obligation.